T0364880

1545

JOHNSTONMARKLEE

Reto Geiser, Editor

HOUSE IS A HOUSE IS A HOUSE IS A HOUSE IS A HOUSE

Architectures and Collaborations of

JOHNSTON MARKLEE

Birkhäuser
Basel

Contents

SPECIFIC INDETERMINACY
Reto Geiser

"Too Dumb for New York City, Too Ugly for L.A." This is how Sharon Johnston and Mark Lee have described themselves on the occasion of a number of lectures, riffing on the title of an album by country legend Waylon Jennings. And, more recently, they reflected on their role within contemporary architectural discourse by paraphrasing Bryan Ferry's lyrics: "We're Too Young to Reason, Too Grown Up to Dream."[1] What may initially appear to be an uneasy relationship between established cultural and generational poles is, in fact, the wellspring of Johnston Marklee's approach to architecture, and their reluctance to assume a singular perspective is the manifestation of something more interesting and complex.

Educated in the United States, with academic teaching experience in Europe, Johnston Marklee are based in Los Angeles and maintain strong cultural connections around the world. They are representative of a generation that cut itself loose from the polemical positions of its precursors and they have discovered limitless opportunities in this freedom.[2] Unconcerned with disciplinary ideologies, and with the ways in which others would position their practice within them, Johnston Marklee are committed to making a direct and tangible contribution to the built environment.[3] Despite the loose fit of their work relative to established trends and frameworks, their practice is deeply rooted in the culture of architecture. Through the reevaluation of modernist dogma and the contamination of known idioms with alien forms and sensibilities, their work operates between divergent poles both within and outside of architecture. By embracing this middle ground as its own category, Sharon Johnston and Mark Lee have succeeded in creating a paradoxical identity; they are at home between the high and the low, the present and the past, the contextual and the autonomous.

Accordingly, this book does not favor a singular point of view, but instead creates a conversation among a variety of interests and approaches as a means to present the recurring themes of their practice. In many ways, *House is a House is a House is a House is a House* marks the end of Johnston Marklee's formative period. Focusing upon five residential projects—as the title's repetition suggests—and including the same number of critical voices and artist's reflections of the work, this publication resists the conventional format of an architectural monograph. It is, rather, an open-ended contemplation of nearly twenty years of architectural experimentation in which the house has served as a testing lab.

HISTORY WITHOUT ECLECTICISM

In the context of Los Angeles, a city characterized by rapid change and redevelopment, Johnston Marklee's deep appreciation of architectural history may seem slightly unusual. In a design milieu preoccupied with formal novelty, emergent technology, and a willful disdain for historicism, a relaxed relationship to precedent runs the risk of appearing anachronistic. Sharon Johnston and Mark Lee, however, are not only as well versed in architectural history as they are in popular culture, but they are also among few in the field who are able to comfortably integrate them without compromising their independence as designers. They acknowledge a wide range of divergent influences on their work and consequently "don't have the impetus at the start of every project to be innovative."[4]

As is the case with many Southern California architects, Johnston Marklee launched their practice with residential projects, continuing the tradition that began with early Modernist experiments in the first decades of the twentieth century, followed by the Case Study House Program shortly after the Second World War. The firm's first project in Los Angeles was to replace a house that had been destroyed in a fire, the structure for which Morphosis's 2-4-6-8 House (1978) had served as an annex. As one of Thom Mayne and Michael Rotondi's first projects built in the heyday of Postmodernism, the house is a simple box with yellow window frames, blue lintels, red scuppers, and a pyramidal roof.[5] Rather than forcing a confrontation with or renunciation of this earlier project, Johnston Marklee recognized its significance and used its history as a starting point for their response. As suggested in one of their diagrams for the project, a conceptual isometric reminiscent of Morphosis's urban ambition, Johnston Marklee's scheme for the Sale House suggests an inversion of the original *parti* that in many ways appears to be a fraternal twin to the 2-4-6-8 House. Despite the fact that the two structures share a continuous plinth and similar proportions, the architectural articulation of the two projects couldn't be more different. Through the strategic placement of windows to create a dynamically unbalanced composition, and the use of highly saturated colors for interior spaces contrasted by a muted grey exterior, Johnston Marklee depart from the platonic geometry, symbolic elements, and primary colors of the existing structure, and they thereby challenge its iconic character. By reflecting the existing context conceptually, rather than figuratively, Johnston Marklee enlist close formal observation informed by historical knowledge to create a distinctive and contemporary architectural response.

Architectural representation not only informed the conception of this project, but it also significantly influenced its public reception. In "House for Sale," a series of photographs commissioned by the architects to document the Sale House, the photographer Livia Corona alludes to the role of architectural imagery and especially the theatricality of the project's postmodern heritage. In her photographs, she staged a group of elderly people, dressed to match with or contrast the intense color shades of pink, turquoise and yellow-orange applied to the interior volumes of the house. Deliberately clashing the abstract and neutral shades of white and grey with the lively, oversaturated colors and surreal scenes that unfold within the house, this hyperaesthetic yet ironic representation of Johnston Marklee's project stresses the reversal of the original scheme and substantiates the amalgamation of past and present in their work.

In keeping with today's media-driven world, Johnston Marklee has sustained an ongoing interest in elaborate forms of representation throughout their work. Photographic collaborations such as those presented in this book are evidence of the architects' interest in pushing the limits of architectural representation, while refraining from the prevalent architectural eye-candy facilitated by current rendering techniques. Instead, they reappropriate the technique of collage, as it was used to shape architectural representation in the early twentieth century. Frequently assembled through the composition of historical pictures—the crowds in front of Giuseppe Terragni's Casa del Fascio in Como—or film stills—including a view of Adalberto Libera's Villa Malaparte as staged in Jean-Luc Godard's 1963 *Le Mépris*—these artifacts not only serve as a means to document and disseminate the work, but also provide a cultural-historical background for it.

A

B

C

A   Johnston Marklee, Hill House, Los Angeles,
    2004, collage with Julius Shulman's photo-
    graph of Case Study House #22 (24 × 36 in),
    detail.

B   John Baldessari, *Crowd with Shape of Reason
    Missing: Example 1*, 2012, Mixografia print on
    handmade paper (30 × 43 in), detail.

C   Johnston Marklee, Gran Traiano Art Complex,
    Stack House, Grottaferrata, Italy, 2007, col-
    lage with the photograph of a crowd in front
    of the Casa del Fascio, Como (35.5 × 32.55 in).

This approach has its origins in the design for the Hill House, a project located in Pacific Palisades near a number of well-known mid-century case study houses. In the process of designing it, Johnston Marklee adopted Julius Shulman's iconic nighttime photograph of Case Study House #22 by Pierre Koenig (who taught Lee at the University of Southern California). Rather than adding additional layers of visual information to the photograph, the architects subtracted white areas from the image of the existing house to represent the building mass of their proposal. By retouching the cantilevered roof and the hovering floor slab—both of which are prominent in Shulman's picture—they emphasize the house's relationship to its hillside site and its view of the sprawling city unfolding below. More than a simple means of visual communication, this collage combines a cultural-historical model with a contemporary experiment with form to manifest the ambition of the project. By means of visual aggregation, the architects locate architectural history at the core of their work and establish an exchange with protagonists from the past.

The material quality of Johnston Marklee's hand-crafted collages suggests a strong affinity with representational practices developed and perfected by such architects as Ludwig Mies van der Rohe in the early twentieth century. The contrast between hard line drawings on a white background, colored photographic elements, and reproductions of art works, recalls the dissolution of interior architectural space in Mies's representation of the Resor House (1938), one of his first American projects.[6] While Johnston Marklee's collages aren't necessarily unique as images, it is curious to trace how the adjustment of historical precedent is made productive in their work. Rather than enact a nostalgic recreation of a Miesian collage, Johnston Marklee reconsider Mies' approach. Similar to the artist John Baldessari's *Crowd with Shape of Reason Missing* (2012), the crisp, white, geometric surfaces that characterize their projects are redacted from a layered background composed of photographic references and colored paper. Instead of defining their intervention in detail, they leave the architectural object blank. It is liberated from a sense of materiality and scale and alludes to the autonomy of the project. This representational technique might subdue the plasticity that is characteristic for most of Johnston Marklee's projects, but by dematerializing the architectural image of the project through a kind of meta-abstraction, it equally reinforces their predilection for shape and edge over surface and construction. The collages are consequently more than a particular choice of architectural representation. They serve as working images in the design process and as post-facto presentation drawings at once.

CONTEXT WITHOUT REFERENCE

From their earliest unrealized projects, such as the Scope House and the Mound House, to more recent schemes such as the Round House and the Chile House, Johnston Marklee make prolific use of diagrams. Typically based on parallel projection, the diagrams illustrate austere, solitary objects as viewing devices that frame the scenic, (sub)urban, or cultural context of their projects.[7] From sculptural skylights, to punched holes, to retractable curtain walls, openings and void-spaces are understood to be an integral, three-dimensional feature of the architectural object linking the interior and the exterior of the houses and defining a spatial language for the whole. Additionally, the diagrams provide ways to re-think the notion of *view* and *display* relative to the house typology. But rather than simply framing views of the landscape, a long-standing architectural tradition with origins in landscape painting, Johnston Marklee use the same techniques of graphic redaction and extraction mentioned already to explore new ways to edit and augment the experience of inside/out relationships by accentuating some views and "blanking out" others entirely.

The View House is predicated precisely upon the potential of such oscillation between different conceptions of viewing and display. By joining the liberating views of the Argentinian Pampas to the obstructed environment of a developing suburban neighborhood, the architecture challenges its surrounding context formally in order to amplify the glimpses of the landscape between prospective residences. As Nicolás Valentini's film stills document, the house, through the careful manipulation of light, volume and views, responds to its context through an interior promenade arranged along a continuous sequence of precisely placed apertures and culminating in a mirador, while nevertheless appearing as a solitary figure in the open field.

When considering Johnston Marklee's work out of context, one could have the impression that it is encapsulated in a bubble of architectural autonomy, privileging space over place and ignoring local particularities. But a closer look reveals that most of their buildings are as concerned with their surroundings as they are with their own formal operations and, in many cases, actually redefine their contexts in ways that render conventional distinctions between the "formal" and "contextual" impossible. For example, in the design for the Hill House in Pacific Palisades the architects balanced a demanding set of zoning parameters (the requirement for new construction to follow the contours of the hill), with the physical constraints of an uneven slope, and the client's desire to maximize the house's volume in the most affordable way possible.

The diagrammatic character of the Hill House reflects a specific moment in the disciplinary dialog that was sparked with a design charrette for the extension of the Museum of Modern Art in New York in 1997.[8] Though none of the proposals—by Herzog & de Meuron, Steven Holl, and OMA—that creatively explored the New York Zoning Resolution were selected, the output of this pivotal selection process under the auspices of curator Terence Riley left its traces on later projects of some of the contenders and beyond.[9] OMA's Seattle Public Library (1999–2004), to name just one example completed in the same year as the Hill House, is one of the most contextual buildings in the city, despite its iconic character with an envelope adapted by particular urban conditions, the framing of specific views, and the modulation of daylight.

Following a similar approach, one could argue that by turning the bureaucratic Hillside Ordinance from a policing device into a productive, form-generating opportunity, Johnston Marklee maximized the building volume while minimizing its footprint, performing a formal transformation clearly visible in the tapered geometry of the project.[10] This intense engagement with context and form led to a redefinition of the front of the house in the hillside: Rather than facing the street, it is now overlooking the Santa Monica Canyon. The main living room acts as if it was part of a thickened building envelope. As can be observed in Veronika Kellndorfer's photographs documenting the Hill House,

D

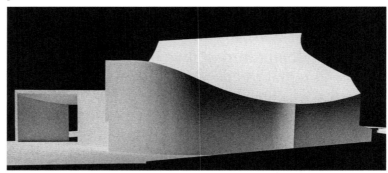

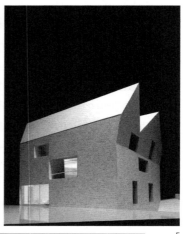

E   F

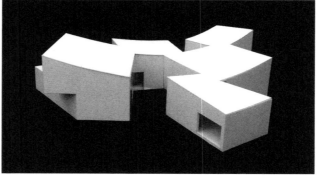

G

D Ernst Gisel, Catholic Church St. Etienne,
   La Sallaz, Switzerland, 1967, model
   (Photo: Georg Gisel).

E Johnston Marklee, Scope House, Ann Arbor,
   Michigan, 1999, model.

F Johnston Marklee, House House, Ordos,
   Inner Mongolia, China, 2008, model.

G Johnston Marklee, Gran Traiano Art Complex,
   Gallery, Grottaferrata, Italy, 2007, model.

large sliding windows allow the space to open diagonally and support an active mediation between the interior and the exterior.

AUTONOMY WITHOUT ISOLATION

The source of architectural forms is far less essential to Johnston Marklee than spatial properties and performative qualities. Responding directly to the prevalent formal experiments in California—exemplified by figures including Frank Gehry, Eric Owen Moss and Greg Lynn, and promoted by institutions such as SCI-Arc and UCLA—Johnston Marklee takes geometry as a tool rather than an end in itself. For instance, their fascination with complex curvature is explored more through Boolean operations than it is through parametric computation. While the office takes advantage of contemporary computational practice, their projects could also have been designed with traditional representational means. The Scope House, for example, is based on a simple lofting action between a horizontal and a vertical rectangle. It is not modeled with complex surface calculation but was conceived by means of a physical paper model. Deliberately distancing themselves from the computation-centered "parametric school," Johnston Marklee approach geometry in a somewhat archaic fashion that uses aesthetic reduction and "crudeness" as the foundation for a formal vocabulary that has driven the practice over the course of the last two decades.

The View House is a development of the geometric principles established in some of Johnston Marklee's earliest design schemes and first tested in a number of smaller projects for the Lannan Foundation in Marfa, Texas. Similar to the Hill House, the project denies the traditional orientation and four-sidedness of the suburban villa and favors instead a dynamic and continuous elevation that both reflects the building's dialog with the surrounding landscape and enforces its formal autonomy. The tectonic complexity of the project is based on the simple subtraction of four spherical domes from the corners of a primitive mass. This is also reflected in the materiality of the building. The formwork of this cast-in-place concrete structure posed serious geometric limitations, to which primitive forms best lent themselves. The repeated application of fragments of spherical formwork, to which local builders were well attuned, allowed the architects to realize this compact yet complex mass. Johnston Marklee are repeatedly negotiating the middle ground between modern abstraction and sculptural expression. Similar to Swiss architect Ernst Gisel, to whose work the architects must have been exposed while teaching in Zurich, abstraction is not treated as mere reduction but understood, instead, as a form of masking. While Gisel considered the design of churches, for example his 1967 proposal for St. Etienne in La Sallaz, as a testing ground for a sculptural-architectural dimension of architecture, Johnston Marklee established their recognizable formal vocabulary through the design of houses. Through the decomposition of known archetypes (such as the cubic mass of the Chile House or the cylindrical mass of the Round House and the View House) and their translation into a conglomerate of architectural elements, form is defamiliarized to allow for multiple readings of the built projects. As a result, the View House is simultaneously blunt and enigmatic; it appears equally crude and sophisticated. At times it resembles a rock, partially sunken into the ground, while at other times it reflects the lightness of a cardboard model accidentally tumbled to the floor.

This delicate equilibrium between lightness and mass recurs in the work of Johnston Marklee and is embodied most strikingly in the Vault House, a beach house on the shore of the Pacific Ocean composed of a number of extruded, telescoped vaults. Its exterior, constrained in a box, contrasts with a virtuosic interior. "In Western architecture," Rem Koolhaas noted, "there has been the humanistic assumption that it is desirable to establish a moral relationship between the two [inside and outside], whereby the exterior makes certain revelations about the interior that the interior corroborates."[11] Following the postmodernist attempt to challenge this assumption by breaking up the dialectic between inside and outside, in the Vault House the fundamental separation of interior from exterior forms relieves the relational constraints between the singular exterior volume from multiple interior volumes.[12] This dialectic between the interior and the exterior seems symbolic, too, of how the firm's practice oscillates between building cultures on either side of the Atlantic. While volume and mass play a central role in Johnston Marklee's conception of space, the apparent solidity of some projects is challenged by their lightweight construction. This also explains the seemingly counterintuitive construction method of the Vault House. Conceived as a series of vaulted spaces hollowed out of a solid mass, this building would, in a European context, most likely have been constructed from a monolithic material—or, due to the related cost constraints, not at all. Consistent with typical American residential construction, however, the ostensibly heavy vaults are framed with wood studs and clad with plasterboard and sheetrock to conceal the crude character of the structural and mechanical systems beneath, thereby divorcing the actual construction process from the notion of carved space upon which the design is founded.

Part-to-whole relationships are decisive in the design of Johnston Marklee's projects. Most of the volumetric configurations are derived from a process of geometric multiplication or subtraction. From View House, to Kauai House, Chile House, and House House, the process of hollowing out space from a building mass is a recurring theme that is particularly evident in the Vault House, where the interior is modulated by the impression of a subtracted volume. As James Welling's photographs of the interior of Porch House highlight, this process is used to define vertical and horizontal apertures, and at times larger void spaces, that are characteristic of Johnston Marklee's interiors in general. In a number of projects, walls are sculpted by contiguous apertures that not only channel natural light into the core of the spaces but also reveal thickness so as to challenge a perception of the projects' compactness. The process of carving also affects the geometry of the apertures and amplifies the graphic effect of figuration on the exterior. This perception of buildings as characters can not only be traced in a great number of white foam core study models that populate the office of Johnston Marklee, but also and equally in photographic representations of their built work—most clearly in diagonal views—as Walead Beshty suggests in his picture narrative that brings to life a group of cartoon-like building caricatures, including Hill House, View House, and Vault House.

The multiplication of self-similar elements is repeatedly deployed as a design strategy in Johnston Marklee's projects. Doubling, for example, is implemented in the Ark House, an addition to Richard Neutra's Sten-Franke-House in Pacific Palisades. The characteristics of the sunroom are duplicated to form a guesthouse, which emphasizes the peculiarities of the existing modernist structure, including its

H

I

J

K

H   Johnston Marklee, Pavilion of Six Views,
    Shanghai, China, 2013.

I   Johnston Marklee, View House, Rosario,
    Argentina, 2009, interior.

J   Johnston Marklee, Menil Drawing Institute,
    Houston, Texas, 2012–17, "Living Room."

K   Johnston Marklee, Menil Drawing Institute,
    Houston, Texas, 2014, collage (27.9 × 21 cm).

curvilinear geometry and the ribbon windows. Court House, a project for a residential housing complex overlooking Lake Geneva, combines elements of both additive and subtractive modes of creating space: semi-public courtyards that structure the building mass can also be read as an aggregation of cubes. Mirroring is another strategy used to define architectural space through a process of multiplication and a focus on interstitial space. The Chile House in Penco, for example, is based on two identical fragments of an ellipsis. The elliptical shapes of the exterior courtyard, which is oriented toward the sky, and the gallery, which stresses the horizontality of the coastline, enhance the perception of the asymmetry of what appears from the exterior to be a singular mass.

The aggregation of fundamental volumes into larger building complexes has repeatedly served as a formal strategy to address the shift from residential projects to an institutional scale. From the gallery, creative offices, and the residential development at the Gran Traiano Art Complex in Grottaferrata, to the competition entry for the Hong Kong Design Institute, or the Pavilion of Six Views in Shanghai, a number of the firm's larger projects oscillate between the appearance of a single building and a series of independent entities linked together. This approach is most evident in the design for the Menil Drawing Institute (MDI), which is currently under construction in Houston. The project mediates the scale between the bungalows of the neighborhood and the Menil Collection museum building designed by Renzo Piano (1981–87) by unifying discrete programmatic volumes under one roof. Connected by a public "living room" and separated by three courtyards, the exhibition spaces and study rooms maintain a domestic scale, which can also be sensed in the modest single-story section of the building.

As outlined in their manifesto-like "Five Points for an Architecture of Approximation," Sharon Johnston and Mark Lee have identified "approximation" as a Trojan horse to reconcile the gap between opposing forces, diverging positions, and conflicting scales.[13] As a sequence of crude and abstract renderings of elevations, published in conjunction with the manifesto suggests, the latitude resulting from this process is what characterizes the work of the office. This cohesive and scale-less representation of sixteen projects not only indicates a

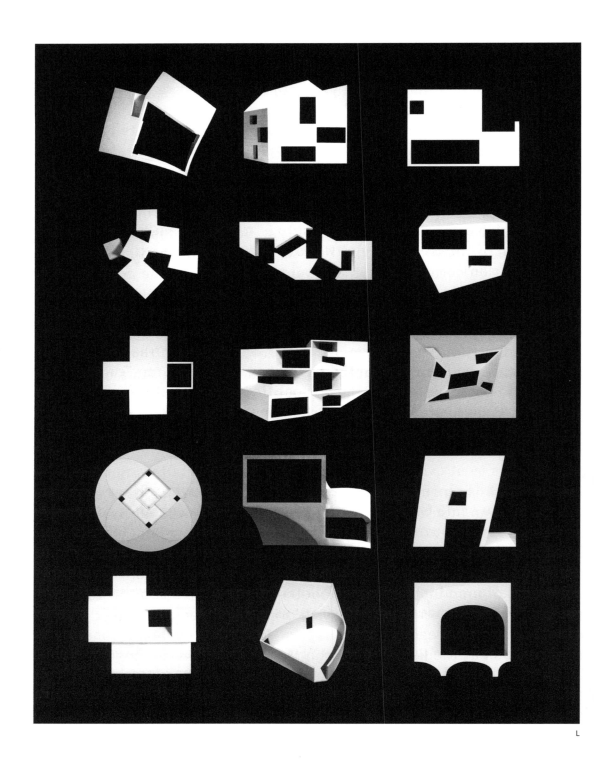

L

L   Johnston Marklee, Alphabet, 2013.

formal vocabulary that is consistent throughout the work of Johnston Marklee, but it also suggests an approach that values similarity over sameness, and one that offers to expand the possibilities of contemporary architecture through a process of approximation.

NETWORKS WITHOUT DEPENDENCE

In a number of conversations and interviews, the firm's principals stressed the importance of finding opportunities to build on a larger scale in other countries in order to be entrusted with projects of a more extensive scope in the United States. But while it is undoubtedly a challenge for most emerging offices to be awarded significant institutional design commissions, there were other reasons the architects sought work abroad. Johnston Marklee's background makes it impossible to overlook their intentional dissociation from the gray eminences of the California school.[14] The architects also suggest a growing dissatisfaction with the detachment of theory from practice as they observe it in the context of American academia. As a consequence, their practice has formed close ties with a group of young and ambitious architects (particularly from Europe and Latin America), who practice, build, and teach, eluding the split between thinking and making.

In their effort to explore new opportunities, the practice has begun to establish an international network of colleagues, who, according to Johnston and Lee, are more open to a mutual exchange and allow them to practice through collaboration. This group was first consolidated in the context of the Ordos 100 project, curated by Ai Weiwei in 2008. The group of architects brought together by the Chinese artist to propose one hundred schemes for lavish private residences in the desert of Inner Mongolia reads like a blueprint for future collaborations.[15] A closer look at the list of Johnston Marklee's works suggests that a series of projects started to take shape in the aftermath of this architectural gathering, many of them initiated by or also involving some of the participants of the Ordos project. Over the years, Johnston Marklee have become participants in a wide-reaching global network of architects. As part of Christian Bourdais' Solo Houses project, they designed Round House in Cretas, Spain; in La Tour-de-Peilzat at Lake Geneva, Switzerland, they contributed a project to a master plan by

Christ & Gantenbein, alongside some of their Ordos peers, including Tatiana Bilbao, Alejandro Aravena, Office KGDVS, and Atelier Bow Wow; in Penco they were invited by Pezo Von Ellrichshausen to design a gallery and courtyard as part of a series of pavilions to launch the post-earthquake reconstruction efforts along the Chilean coastline; and in Grottaferrata, Italy, they invited HHF Architects and Topotek 1 to collaborate on the Grand Traiano Art Complex.

Johnston and Lee's active role in the formation of the Depart Foundation, just outside of Rome, not only stresses their continuous involvement in the design of spaces for the arts—their list of clients includes major institutions such as the the Menil Collection in Houston and the Museum of Contemporary Art in Chicago—but also embodies their interest in the arts as a discipline that can contribute to their own practice. With Walead Beshty, they closely collaborated on *Later Layer*, an exhibition that proposed a dialog between two bodies of work by displaying artworks along with architectural drawings and models in a site-specific installation.[16] With the fashion and design studio BLESS, they collaboratively taught students in Berlin and Karlsruhe. In this instance teaching served as a testing ground to advance their shared belief in sidestepping the conventional definitions of their own disciplines in order to enhance the intersections between fashion, art, design, and architecture.

The majority of visual contributions to this publication are the outcome of ongoing exchanges between the architects and a group of exceptional artists invited to reflect on selected works. Luisa Lambri, for example, frames a detail of the Hill House in a series of abstract photographs that might appear to be identical at first glance. Through this focus on a small segment of the building, she alludes to its geometry and materiality and takes advantage of the surface as a sensitive canvas that allows for the documentation of almost imperceptible changes of light, the transformation of shadows, and subtle variations of color.[17] Jack Pierson's staging of the Vault House stresses the project's strong sculptural quality in the glare of the sun and emphasizes its oscillating silhouette against the bright blue sky. The sequence of views looking out of the house, past a scaffolding, and with a green hose left behind in the loggia, counters the abstract notion of the exterior and conveys an uncanny sense of inhabitation. Marianne Mueller introduces her own perception of the office, as well as its surroundings, in a collection of immersive spreads that serve as an extended book cover to acquaint the reader with the cultural context of the office. Through this visual narrative, the artist not only provides a form of feedback, but also the setting in which Johnston Marklee's work becomes part of her own photographic studies. The architects previously collaborated with Mueller on the site-specific installation *Any House is a Home* (2011–12), a twisting, two-story ziggurat that serves as display for an intuitive selection of archival images and photography by the artist. At first glance, the formation of stacked volumes is undoubtedly reminiscent of other works of Johnston Marklee. But looking more closely, the unconventional spatial arrangement of photographs consistently follows the approach of Mueller's work and allows a more associative and intuitive reading of the artifacts. And the application of photographs onto this sculptural object challenges its geometrical reading and encourages speculation about the relationship between physical and projected space.

Johnston Marklee have a strong affinity for a number of disciplines, but their own way of looking at the world is decisively shaped by the lens of architecture. The architects consistently use the knowledge of associated areas of expertise to enhance spatial practice. They have repeatedly built for artists, including, for example, recent studio interiors for Sterling Ruby, and for art institutions, including among others the Lannan Foundation in Marfa. As an integral part of their design practice, however, Johnston and Lee also invite artists, photographers, and fashion designers, as well as historians, writers, and critics, as sparring partners with whom to collaborate on projects. They learn from diverging disciplinary knowledge, reflect their own work through the lens of others, and use their findings to challenge their own methods and techniques.

Key in all of Johnston Marklee's cooperations is the acknowledgment of each party's autonomy. Not unlike their informed, yet loose relationship to historical precedent, collaborations are understood as flexible relationships that allow the office to enter unknown territories while maintaining the status of outsiders. In this sense, the act of teaming

M

N

O

P

M Johnston Marklee, Office, Los Angeles,
   California, 2011 (Photo: Lindsay Erickson).

N Johnston Marklee, Office, Los Angeles,
   California, 2015 (Photo: James Welling).

O Johnston Marklee, Office, Los Angeles,
   California, 2015 (Photo: James Welling).

P Johnston Marklee, Office, Los Angeles,
   California, 2011 (Photo: Lindsay Erickson).

up does not inevitably lead to an obliteration of authorship but on the contrary facilitates what Johnston and Lee describe as a productive isolation. This book is the outcome of such a collaboration. And while it brings together a great number of individual perspectives, shared interests, and diverging interpretations to spark a process of reflection, it also stresses the integrity of an ambitious and identifiable oeuvre.

GENEROSITY
An allusion to Gertrude Stein's 1913 poem "Sacred Emily," the title of this book not only refers to the specifics of type, scale, character and the number of projects discussed, but it also stresses a deliberately indeterminate dimension that leads to the projects' cohesion as a body of work. Stein confronted literary convention by redefining the use of language, syntax, and narrative order; Johnston Marklee are challenging preconceived categorizations of their work, embracing the concept of approximation as a projective model to mediate between sometimes conflicting poles to suggest new possibilities for architecture. Their projects have been repeatedly labeled—called alternately minimal, austere, aloof, even dumb—but none of these tags seem fitting. Johnston Marklee's approach is rooted in an exceptional intellectual, cultural, and architectural generosity. They embrace a "both-and" attitude, rather than an "either/or" approach, and they work in a process of reverse editing, one of critical accumulation rather than acute reduction.

An outcome of this approach, *House is a House is a House is a House is a House* does not blatantly proclaim a singular position or demarcate territorial lines. But despite its conscious blurring of positions between actors and commentators, its oscillation between contemplation and proclamation, and foundation on a multiplicity of visual displays and textual contributions—including the voices of the protagonists themselves—this book is not merely a collection of over a decade of Johnston Marklee's architectural explorations. It is rather an effort to identify the architect's attitude toward practice and their position within architectural discourse. In their work, Johnston Marklee identify constraints as possibilities and strike an astonishing balance between absolute control and laissez-faire. They sidestep time by embracing history without nostalgia, and by considering what *will be* without

losing their grounding. Their work is at the same time formal and contextual. It is concurrently autonomous and engaged. As the visual
and written accounts in this book underline, Sharon Johnston and
Mark Lee's projects escape blunt categorization—their transgression
of boundaries is strategic, their indeterminacy specific.

Notes

1. "Too Dumb for New York, Too Ugly for L.A.," lecture first presented at Syracuse University, New York, 2007; "Too Young to Reason, Too Grown Up to Dream," lecture at Rice University, School of Architecture, February 2012. The latter is a line paraphrased from Bryan Ferry's 1985 all-time hit "Slave to Love."

2. In her exhibition and publication *Everything Loose Will Land*, Sylvia Lavin frames looseness as a potential to rethink the field of operation of architecture and to "loosen up the expectations what architecture should be." See: Sylvia Lavin, *Everything Loose Will Land: 1970s Art and Architecture in Los Angeles*, (Nürnberg: Verlag für moderne Kunst): 21–23.

3. See also: Reto Geiser, Sharon Johnston, Mark Lee (eds.), *Later Layer: Johnston Marklee and Walead Beshty* (Grottaferrata: Depart Foundation, 2010): 31.

4. See for example: "Johnston Marklee (Postopolis! LA)," accessed March 12, 2013. http://www.cityofsound.com/blog/2009/06/johnston-marklee-postopolis-la.html.

5. See also: "2-4-6-8 House," accessed March 14, 2013. http://morphopedia.com/projects/2-4-6-8-house.

6. In the collages for the Resor House for example, Mies montaged Paul Klee's *Colorful Meal* (1928) as well as the scenery of the site along the Snake River in Wyoming's Grand Teton Mountains.

7. On architecture as a viewing device see also: Martino Stierli, "Architectures of Projection," in Moisés Puente (ed.), *2G*, No. 67, Johnston Marklee (Barcelona: Editorial Gustavo Gili, 2013): 4–10.

8. John Elderfield (ed.), *Studies in Modern Art 7: Imagining the Future of the Museum of Modern Art* (New York: Harry N. Abrams/The Museum of Modern Art, 1998).

9. In the "Evolution of a City Building Under the Zoning Law," Hugh Ferriss describes zoning laws as a form-making device rather than a restriction. Hugh Ferriss, "The New Architecture," in *The New York Times Magazine*, March 19 (1922): 8–9. Terence Riley was, coincidentally, a member of the jury that recognized the Hill House with a 2002 Progressive Architecture (P/A) Award.

10. See also: Mark Lee, "Liberating and Governing Mechanisms," in *San Rocco 4: "Fuck Concepts! Context!,"* (Milan: San Rocco, 2012): 105–111.

11. Rem Koolhaas, *Delirious New York: A Retroactive Manifesto for Manhattan* (New York: Oxford, 1978): 82.

12. For the postmodernist dialectic between interior and exterior, see: Frederic Jameson, "Architecture and the Critique of Ideology," in *The Ideologies of Theory: Essays 1971–1986*, vol. 2 (Minneapolis: University of Minnesota Press, 1988): 59.

13. Sharon Johnston and Mark Lee, "Generic Specificity: Five Points for an Architecture of Approximation," in Moisés Puente (ed.), *2G*, No. 67, Johnston Marklee (Barcelona: Editorial Gustavo Gili, 2013): 166–175.

14. Sharon Johnston studied at Stanford University, Mark Lee at the University of Southern California (USC) in Los Angeles.

15. Reto Geiser, "In the Realm of Architecture: Some Notes on Ai Weiwei's Spatial Temptations," in Yilmaz Dziewior (ed.), *Ai Weiwei: Art/Architecture* (Bregenz: Kunsthaus Bregenz, 2011): 38–40. On Johnston Marklee's international network see also: Christopher Hawthorne, "On the Inside Looking Out," in *Architect*, November (2012): 76.

16. *Later Layer*, Exhibition at the Italian Cultural Institute, Los Angeles, January 16 to February 28, 2010.

17. On Luisa Lambri see: Matthew Drutt, *Luisa Lambri: Locations* (Houston: The Menil Collection): 12–36.

A)

Sale House
Venice
California
2004

Portrait

Livia Corona

I)

On Totality

Mark Lee in conversation with

Philip Ursprung

PU   There is an art-historical tradition of claiming that the totality of the works, the oeuvre, is more than just the sum of its parts. The tradition has its roots in early nineteenth-century Romanticism and today is perhaps most prominently exemplified by Gerhard Richter's career. Most observers identify his oeuvre with his life and assume that the entire oeuvre is coherent, driven by an inner logic. From the very beginning of his career Richter himself has promoted this interpretation, giving numbers to every single work of art and thereby suggesting that they are evolving continuously and not simply added as parts of a series. The same was the case earlier in the twentieth century, for Paul Klee. In the realm of architecture, I would claim Herzog & de Meuron as part of this tradition. Each of their projects carries within itself the memory of the oeuvre as well as the potential of future works. Some even bear names: as if they were actors in a play that takes place within the frame of the architect's career. What about your own practice? Do you feel part of this tradition?

ML   We are aware of the importance of an oeuvre in one's work but we also see the pitfalls of being too self-conscious about it. At the outset of our practice, we said we did not want to be like the previous generation of architects whom often had recourse to one particular style, one recognizable signature as a surrogate for ideology. But after practicing for a certain amount of time and looking back at our body of work, we realized that there are certain recurring tendencies and preoccupations, such as the interrelationship between mass, weight, and aperture, that we tended to wrestle with over and over again even though the impetus behind each project was fresh and innocent. We are always looking at what a project is and how it could inform our work: "How could architecture contribute to this new problem and in this new situation?" We are not following a top-down approach. This makes sense for us because it prevents intellectual sclerosis and adds value to our understanding.

ML   A few years ago, we had a discussion in Los Angeles addressing the relationship between art and architecture. Comparing this relationship in both Herzog & de Meuron and Frank Gehry's practices, you said in the former's work the separation between disciplines is clear and distinct. And you said that because they have a clear stance on the differences between fields they have the liberty to "steal" from artists, whether direct techniques or conceptual frameworks. Regarding Frank Gehry, on the other hand, you suggested his work aspires to be sculpture—in the way that his Chiat Day building is competing with Claes Oldenburg's binoculars. This is a very fundamental distinction for us, something that

ART OR ARCHITECTURE?

Frank Gehry, Chiat/Day/Mojo Office (also known as the Binoculars Building), Venice, California, 1985–91.

we repeatedly have been trying to articulate. We have been thinking about the relationship between architecture and art ever since starting our office, and we have been trying to find answers by directly engaging in collaborations with artists and dialogs with thinkers in the art world.

PU I would not say that the goal of the individual project, in your case, is to realize something that can succeed in the realm of art or that can compete with works of art. Nevertheless I would locate your work in a tradition of architects who consider architecture as a part of art. Your approach is perhaps more relaxed because these definitions have generally become less substantial for our generation.

ML So how would you frame our position within a larger trajectory of this relationship between art and architecture?

PU At the beginning of Herzog & de Meuron's career it was important to defend the autonomy of architecture because architecture as such had lost so much ground during the late nineteen-sixties and early seventies. From their point of view, architecture around 1970 had degenerated to a mere appendix of other fields such as sociology, politics, and economics. It had lost its physical presence and became a phantom. Then they discovered a way out of the dilemma. They felt, as did many young architects of their generation, that they could reanimate architecture by means of the rhetoric of Aldo Rossi, who defended the autonomy of architecture. Of course, his claim that "architecture is architecture" related to the much earlier idea of "l'art pour l'art"—and therefore echoed an inherently artistic logic. However, his ideas did allow the younger generation a new start; it was no wonder he was the most cherished teacher during the seventies and eighties on both sides of the Atlantic.

Toward the end of the nineteen-eighties this problem was solved. Architecture returned to solid ground and this renewed stability clarified its relation to art. To use a metaphor that was popular during the eighties, namely that of the artist as boxer, one could claim that architects looked to artists as sparring partners, not in order to mimic them or become artists themselves but in order to improve their own technique and make architecture stronger and better. This is what fascinated Herzog & de Meuron for more than a decade. The art world—with its exhibitions, its critics, its curiosity and openness—was an ideal testing ground for their projects. It allowed their work to resonate much more than in the architecture world, which was, at that time, much more inert.

ML Working in the American context, I see some parallels within the discipline itself, maybe different from what Herzog & de Meuron experienced when sociology and politics were overwhelming architecture and when resorting to Aldo Rossi and typology became a defense mechanism. We've noticed, as we engage with the American academic context, that there is a notion that both digital developments and theory have taken architecture to the point of detachment from practice. We are therefore interested in finding an irreducible domain of what the boundaries of architecture are by adopting less of a militant pose, simply because one could argue that the problem of the digital arose from within the discipline itself. But to get back to your sparring partner analogy: we think artists are doing a lot of work that is not encumbered by what we do as architects. And they often come up with the most interesting and unexpected responses to problems. What are the differences you see between the architectural world and the art world, particularly in academia?

PU One of the problems that exists in the context of the United States is that in architecture, you sort of lack sparring partners—or they are always the same three figures. It is always about Peter Eisenman and his heritage and network and then there are only maybe three possible moves. I am exaggerating and simplifying here, but I think there has been quite an orthodox, academic, normative frame. Like a chess game but with only two chessmen left; there are not so many moves that you can make. So, for me, it is evident that you take into play other figures, players who are not the usual suspects, the father figures sanctioned by academe. And, despite the fact that it has opened up a lot during the last decade, the world of architecture is perhaps still less accessible, experimental, and playful than the art world, in which the old national boundaries no longer exist.

ML It seems fair to state this in regards Peter Eisenman's generation. It evidently goes back to Colin Rowe and Robert Slutzky's obsession with painting, a type of reading from a Cubist painting. But there are examples where the techniques or the comprehension of art in their direct translation into architecture actually suffocated rather than liberated it. For example, Bernhard Hoesli's interpretation of Rowe and Slutzky's "Transparency," which further confounded the problems inherent in their essay, in particular the insistence on flatness as a prelude to reading and cognition. It runs the risk of focusing exclusively on the reduced representations of plans and sections as a basis of reading. Their inclination for frontal pictorial readings presupposes a predominant linear axis in order to allow the play of shallow space to be read. This is an example whereby directly transplanting the technique of one discipline into another is problematic. If you take the values from another discipline directly into architecture, it becomes an academic norm. Painting has been exhausted as a means and reference for architecture. We are trying to think

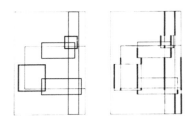

Transparency exercise from Bernhard Hoesli's design studio at ETH Zurich, ca. 1965, based on Colin Rowe and Robert Slutzky's essay "Transparency" (1963).

about other possibilities for architecture through art beyond painting.

PU   It is certainly a challenge for your practice that you do not have so many interlocutors. Your buildings are like kids in a neighborhood where there are no other kids—you have to imagine your playmates. And that might be one of the reasons why you feel quite comfortable in the desert, for example. There is nobody around, so you do not miss anybody. This stands probably in contrast to an art world that is, I think, characterized by many interlocutors almost everywhere.

ML   Beyond technique and discourse, the relationship between architecture and art also has a lot to do with the exchange value between cultural capital. I remember Rafael Moneo commented on the insecurity of American architects, that they have to latch onto a cultural norm to validate themselves. But beyond cultural hierarchies, there is an economic value to this. Moneo claims it was when Frank Gehry noticed that while Robert Rauschenberg's dirt painting was composed without great means, the amount of money and the resources invested into preserving it was exponential because of its status as art. And, through this example, he understood that the way for architecture to transcend the value system of real estate was to enter into the value system of another realm; when architecture enters the realm of art, it gains another value.

Robert Rauschenberg, *Dirt Painting (for John Cage)*, ca. 1953, dirt and mold in wood box (39.4 × 40.6 × 6.4 cm), detail.

BEING ONE STEP BEHIND OR ONE STEP AHEAD

PU   It seems that you have been making an effort to set your practice apart from the academic milieu in the United States both by means of collaborating with artists and by working abroad. How has your practice benefited from such encounters?

ML   The contexts for collaborations with artists are typically ephemeral. For example, installation or exhibition design is short, fast, and impermanent. It puts us outside of our box. In such projects, we always approach problems with someone else. In that sense, exhibitions and installations are good sampling platters. We work with artists, scientists, sociologists, fashion designers, and others. They offer us a different type of framework and cadence of thinking and working. They help us look at things in a very different way. And although we work within the American context, we now work more outside this sphere, and have found an audience more sympathetic, more empathetic, to our approach—we've found, to use your metaphor, more friends in the neighborhood. We are not consciously working internationally for the sake of being international, but rather do so to take breaks from the hegemonic cultural construct in the United States. Gabriel Orozco is said to declare that American culture is like a big teenager—decadent, self-indulgent, with a detachment from reality, and very self-focused. So he prefers to be alternately childlike or very mature; he wants to leave out this adolescent middle part. Perhaps our attraction to Europe, South America, and Asia is similar to Orozco's—trying to find something more mature and something very young at the same time. And maybe that is a good way to find a balance between extremes, not a static, averaged-out type of balance but a dynamic one that oscillates between polarities. In the past, we have been asked about our interest in the work being timeless. For us, it's less about being timeless than about being out of time, about being anachronistic. We like being either one step behind or one step ahead. In a way, dynamically engaging the past and the future, as well as the notion of being somewhere else, helps you define where you are, geographically as well as in history and in time.

PU   That might be what we've described as the sadness or old-fashioned sensibility in your work. I think your work expresses a kind of longing for something different—*Sehnsucht*, a hope for something that is not fulfilled at that moment and forces one to step out of and into a different time. And this would, of course, connect you to art because it has a different temporality than architecture.

ML   Do you think that this notion of longing is manifested in the work or, rather, in an attitude? I was thinking back to Aldo Rossi. If there is a kind of melancholy and pessimism in our work, we also aspire to something that is simultaneously joyous, like the way Giorgio de Chirico combined stoic forms with oversaturated colors in his early work. We do not see our work like Rossi in the sense that there is not the same kind of gravitas or prolonged sadness to it, but it is somehow dynamic and fleeting. But could you further extrapolate the notion of melancholy? Take Rossi's Fagnano Olona—is it a melancholic building?

Giorgio de Chirico, *Melancholia*, dated 1916, painted ca. 1940, oil on canvas 20×26.5 in. (50.8×67.3 cm).

Aldo Rossi, Fagnano Olona Elementary School, Varese, Italy, 1972–76.

PU   Yes. Fagnano Olona is, of course, melancholic in the sense that Rossi talks about a disrupted unity, a vanishing industrial past. And Rossi sees the disjunction of the present perhaps as a tragedy. As with Eisenman, the basis is tragic. And for you, or for anyone of your generation, the basis is never tragic. Our time is fine. There is no real problem in that sense. This is a big distinction from the previous generation—look at Hans Kollhoff, for example, whose work also has a tragic basis. Even Herzog & de Meuron still have some kind of tragedy written into their work. Not as much as Kollhoff who, like Gerhard Richter and others of the generations born between 1930 and 1950, have to "heal" the wounds that the war and, later, the country's division inflicted upon Germany. But even for someone raised in postwar Switzerland, such as Jacques Herzog or Pierre de Meuron, the alienation of the subject from its surroundings and the experiences of the rapid economic and social change can still partially be considered tragic. For "baby boomers" who grew up amidst the prosperity of the sixties and early seventies, like you—and like myself—there is no such thing as a tragic precondition. This might be one of the reasons why your work is so experimental, so playful, almost frivolous in the German sense of *frivol*, and not afraid of confronting various issues such as different levels of taste while everything is at hand. So there is nothing tragic. I would rather say there is, perhaps, skepticism about the direction that American architecture has taken, and it could be so much more, it could be so much different. Perhaps this resonates in your work.

ML   On the one hand, times are good now in a way that makes it seems contrived to impose a certain tragic component when none whatsoever, or only very little, exists; it becomes a form of melancholic self-aggrandizement. On the other hand, at least within the American context, there exists an anything-goes mentality and a longing for some containment and grounding within the discipline. For us, the basis of the work is certainly not tragic. So within this anything-goes context, we are trying to find a place of solace, an eye-of-the-storm moment where the chaos around could be ordered. An analogy would be instead of juxtaposing Serlio's tragic and comic settings into a hybrid, to introduce an effect of *Verfremdung* within the comic setting. For example, when we look back at our design process we always have a tendency to shroud the intentions behind the work. When a project has reached a certain degree of development, we sometimes go back and integrate dumber, ham-handed situations into it. We want projects to convey a certain enigmatic quality on the first impression, something that doesn't, say, jump out and announce itself. When you first look at one of our projects it is not obvious what it is doing but, when you spend time looking, the content of the project slowly reveals itself.

PU   This also relates to the mechanisms of postconceptual art, in the sixties and seventies, in which the temporality of the perception is important. You can quickly grasp the idea but then you have a lot of time to explore it. You don't want to sell the whole thing in one explosion.

ML   It broaches on the desire for discreetness and ineffability in the intention behind the work, as well as the fissure between the reception and the production of it. I read once that Ed Ruscha said that "Good art should elicit a response of 'Huh? Wow!' as opposed to 'Wow! Huh?'" His dictum points to the importance of defamiliarization as a prelude to cognition. We try to solicit this type of reception in our projects. However, we often find it in inverse relation to how the work is produced. We tend to start projects with additive rather than reductive processes. We begin by aggregating all the anxieties, everything that needs to be addressed and taken care of. And then, one by one, we find ways to consolidate, veil, and erase until the project is distilled to a state where it oscillates between being familiar and unfamiliar at the same time.

PU   Jeff Koons, in an interview given in the eighties, stated that he always intends to produce works that attract viewers at first glance. Then, it is entirely up to the viewers if they want to enter more deeply into the subject matter. In my view, this is a typically North American attitude. In some sense this double approach—to be attractive at first glance yet to offer the possibility for a "deeper" involvement as well—also applies to your work. The clarity, the beauty, the whiteness makes your models immediately attractive. And, once our attention is captured, we are free to choose what to do. There is something very light about your projects, which I admire. But there is also another side. And, as I said, I would not call it tragic. But perhaps it can be related to the concept of depression, used as a metaphor for a general cultural condition that has prevailed since the nineteen-seventies. The French sociologist Alain Ehrenberg wrote a beautiful book about this; it's entitled *The Weariness of the Self: Diagnosing the History of Depression in the Contemporary Age.* In his view, depression is not only a psychic disease but it is also a symptom of a cultural phenomenon. He states that we have so many choices available that we are stressed, or depressed, by the sheer need to become ourselves. He also states that conflicts have been eradicated and that everybody aims at consent because we have to please each other in order to succeed. The "deconflictualization" forces us to internalize conflicts. If one adapts this concept to your projects, one could claim that, lacking the possibility to enter in conflict with other existing positions, the projects have to focus on themselves and interiorize the conflict. Your affinity for classicism might be related to this trend. Classicism is always about joints and edges, in other words, about points, things that one can hold on to. In a context that is deconflictualized, smooth and slippery, the classicist tradition suddenly becomes attractive because it promises some kind of reference. What Greg Lynn does, for example, is totally different from your approach. His projects seem to submit to the state of deconflictualization. They become mere design.

ML   Although recent research in architecture has generated a set of inquiries into the dissolution of borders and a propensity for smoothness, this trajectory is met by an opposite desire for limits and definition of boundaries. These

POSITIONS

two positions have implications for the way one works with or against rules, from both design and disciplinary standpoints. For example, an architect from the parametric school might place a building within an existing context and, whatever that context is, he or she would begin to morph the context according to the building. For us this becomes a disingenuous way to treat the existing context. We try to be very careful, in our own work, about addressing notions of context. We establish and identify the elements within the context that we deliberately work against very early on in the project, as opposed to categorically working against everything.

PU This means, of course, that the project becomes rather autonomous, in the sense that you establish rules and then play with these rules. Every time there are new rules—this is something that is typical for your work—and, thus, every project is very specific. You don't apply a style. It is a new chapter, even a new language, every time. This might relate to the wholeness, in the sense that it produces a micro- and a macrocosm for every single project. There is a coherence, and you are supposed to participate in the rules of the game, in the language that you establish for this specific project. And this might also have to do with the lack of interlocutors, partners with whom you can discuss.

ML This coherence you refer to inevitably requires a degree of connectivity within each project. But rather than concentrating on the connectivity, we are more interested in boundaries that need to be established in order to enable this connectivity. Our approach can be framed by comparing cross-sections of two theater projects designed four hundred years apart. One is the Teatro Olimpico in Vicenza designed by Andrea Palladio and completed by Vincenzo Scamozzi. The stage and the boundary between the stage and the audience areas are fused into one, so that when you are sitting among the audience you feel as if you were part of the stage. In order to do that, Palladio and Scamozzi had to construct a hard boundary to isolate the interior from the exterior. The boundary is very hard, but once that boundary is established, then the proscenium and the audience area can be fused into one. This stands in contrast to OMA/Rem Koolhaas's Cardiff Bay Opera House project, a cross-section later used again for the Luxor Theater in Rotterdam. This cross-section is made of two volumes; the first is a large box containing the proscenium and the private support spaces. The second is a continuous loop containing the audience area, the public foyer. There is a definitive boundary between the volumes. OMA made no attempts to reconcile the two and they remain incoherent volumes held tangentially in a precarious way. But precisely because of this deliberate separation, a new connectivity was

Andrea Palladio and Vincenzo Scamozzi, Teatro Olimpico, Vicenza, Italy, 1580–85. Longitudinal section drawing by Ottavio Bertotti Scamozzi, 1776.

Office for Metropolitan Architecture (OMA), Cardiff Bay Opera House, Cardiff, Wales, 1994.

enabled and in that continuous loop fused the public foyer and the audience area into one space. And the fusion within the continuous loop is clearly separated from the box where the proscenium, the stage, and the support areas are located. In comparison to Palladio and Scamozzi, there is no exterior boundary between the lobby and the seating areas—except for the occasional separation by a moveable hydraulic wall for performances. But the boundary is defined between the proscenium and the audience. The brilliance of this section lies not in the blurring of every boundary that exists but rather in the strategic and decisive way of shifting where the borders are established so that smoothness could occur.

PU   Koolhaas's approach, in some ways, relates to Mies van der Rohe and to Joseph Paxton, in whose work space is considered to be a system, something that can be assembled and dismantled freely, that can be engineered. You seem to think of space as something more sculptural, closer to the tradition of Hans Scharoun, of Herzog & de Meuron. This kind of spatiality is more organic; one cannot simply subtract or add a module.

ML   Between the organicist spatiality of Palladio, Scharoun, and Herzog & de Meuron and the isolated, recombinable spatiality of Paxton, Mies, and Koolhaas you described, we certainly feel that with our current projects we are at the threshold of moving from the first to the second spatiality. We recently began designing a building for UCLA—graduate art studios—where we have to create a new campus around an existing warehouse. We have been looking at spaces of art production and realized that the best spaces for art production are often quite neutral. We were specifically thinking of Renaissance palaces or nineteenth-century industrial warehouses as the spaces most adaptable to any type of program, spaces that can as easily be a palace or a school for the arts. Lacaton & Vassal's renovation of the Palais de Tokyo in Paris and its particular material approach and type of finish was an important precedent. Another example is Frank Gehry's Temporary Contemporary in Los Angeles, where he reappropriated a warehouse and valorized the essence of neutrality intrinsic to that type of space. The project for UCLA, along with a few other ones, represents a shift in the type of projects in which we are engaged and, subsequently, the spatial thinking behind them: the nature of our projects is changing from the residential to the institutional scale. We are facing new situations and changing demands, things for which the solutions of previous projects might not be appropriate.

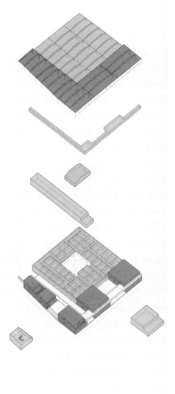

Johnston Marklee, UCLA Graduate Art Studios, Culver City, California, 2011.

Lacaton & Vassal, Palais de Tokyo, Paris, France, 2010–12.

Frank Gehry, Temporary Contemporary, interim exhibition space for the Museum of Contemporary Arts, Los Angeles, California, 1983.

ML   We were recently invited by Terrence Riley to do an installation at the Hong Kong-Shenzhen Biennale. They invited twelve architects to create an installation entitled *The Street*, a direct reference to Paolo Portoghesi's *Strada Novissima* installed at the first Venice Architecture Biennale in 1980, where twenty architects each created a facade to be installed at the Corderie dell'Arsenale. I am very interested in Postmodernism at that very moment, because it was the last gasp, right before Postmodernism became extinct. I myself was educated at a time when Postmodernism in the United States was in the process of fading away. And it very quickly turned into Neomodernism and Deconstructivism and, eventually, into the digital dream or nightmare we've all had to face the last fifteen years. I remember when Postmodernism was waning within the academic context: the Postmodernist architects would invite each other to their own reviews, and they would speak a very closed and codified language that no one else would understand. There was a sense of desperation, like they were holding onto each other hoping to stay afloat a little longer, and they became extinct in a hurry.

Today, the digital school is going through a similar posture. When digital design first emerged, it was full of optimism and bore a very positivistic and democratic vision of what new

BEYOND POSTMODERNISM

Paolo Portoghesi (curator), *Strada Novissima* at the Corderie dell'Arsenale, Venice Biennale, First International Architecture Exhibition, Venice, Italy, 1980.

technology could offer. But in the last five years the discussion among digital architects has largely shifted from the promises of the built environment to the discourse on affect and effects. It turned into an esoteric way of empowering a small group of people to become arbiters of taste. For the purpose of reflection on our own times, I am therefore interested in the moments of Postmodernism and its various predecessors and strains. A lot of people in our generation are trying to go back and reevaluate what we may appreciate about Postmodernism in the work of figures such as Oswald Mathias Ungers, Aldo Rossi, Giorgio Grassi, or James Stirling. All of them were, unfortunately, thrown away with the bathwater.

Jürgen Mayer H., Border Checkpoint, Sarpi, Georgia, 2010–11.

Peter Eisenman, Wexner Center for the Arts, Ohio State University, Columbus, Ohio, 1983–89.

PU That relates very much to what Jürgen Mayer H. thinks about the seventies. He considers the period somehow unfinished. It is almost as if our generation were betrayed by our parents' generation, which prescribed a temporality which was theirs, not ours. Their idea of progress had shaped temporality, although this progress had come to an end with the seventies recession. With the energy crisis of the early seventies, the party was over. Seen from a Marxist perspective, capital could no longer tolerate the rise of wages that had brought prosperity to the middle class after the war. A new round of so-called primitive accumulation took place, by means of the astronomic profits of the petrodollars after the increase of the oil prices in 1973. Productivity was increased by means of the introduction of the computer and the standardized shipping container. On the other hand, the middle class was put under stress by unemployment and the decay of wages, a trend has continued to our own present day. The 1968 revolutions had failed to affect the economic system and remained limited to the realm of culture. Even worse, the intelligentsia "naturalized" the economic crisis by interpreting it as a cultural phenomenon, a shift between two cultural periods, namely "modernism" and "postmodernism." The debate about this shift kept them busy during the seventies and eighties and kept them from analyzing what really had happened. (Interestingly enough, the architects were the first to refuse to discuss these terms.) So not only did our generation inherit our parents' temporality but it also inherited their pseudoconflict, "modern versus postmodern," which blurred the picture of the real economic change. I find David Harvey's idea of linking the economic crisis to a crisis of representation more fruitful than is a dualistic model of interpretation. This resonates in Peter Eisenman's work around the eighties, for instance. His Wexner Center, or the Convention Center of Columbus, Ohio, is much more interesting, in my view, than the later, formalist work, because it is intrinsically related to the crisis of representation and tells us more about the radical changes of the time than does any debate about modernism and postmodernism.

ML   Do you think current interest in Aldo Rossi and James Stirling's generation has to do with a contemporary anxiety for representation?

PU   Yes; I would argue that they go back in time and see where, from their point of view, the wrong road was taken. The advantage of being thrown out of the temporality of our parents' generation in the seventies is that we no longer believe in linear progress. Temporal succession is replaced by spatial juxtaposition. Time is moving more slowly. This allows traveling back in time without being nostalgic or reactionary. One is free to interpret Rossi in a new way.

ML   This is similar to Dave Hickey's narrative of how artists often operate. He said artists look around and say everything sucks. So they go back in history, define the point when they feel things started to decline, and embrace that moment to move forward from there. Similarly, the current generation of architects could wonder about that particular moment in history. And, to many, it would cross the early career of Aldo Rossi. Yoshiharu Tsukamoto of Atelier Bow Wow, for example, said that if he had to paraphrase his architectural project, it would be situated at the intersection of the Metabolists and Aldo Rossi. It is an interesting way to define a position between two seemingly opposite extremes and, rather than finding a static equilibrium between the two, to dynamically oscillate between them to establish one's ground. And for Yoshiharu, the historical moment he embraced was situated when the concern for representation was taking shape. The Metabolists would be right before this crisis of representation, and Rossi would be in the center of it.

Aldo Rossi, Gallaratese Housing Block, Milan, Italy, 1969–73.

PU   Rossi would certainly be at the core of the crisis of representation. He worked in the industrial center of continental Europe, in northern Italy, during the most brutal phase of deindustrialization. Gallaratese, for example, is clearly about the crisis of representation. It embodies an anachronism, the collision of different temporalities. One can hear the hammering of the machines of the industrial age in its segments and already perceive the order of the computers of the information age. It oscillates between a construction site and a ruin, not dead and not alive.

ML   Following what we discussed earlier, about Rossi and Herzog & de Meuron, the field of architecture seems to be losing power as a cultural discourse today. Over the years, many alternative media emerged that seem much more relevant and equipped than architecture is to address cultural changes. They have taken over what architecture once did. I

ARCHITECTURE'S AGENCY

don't know if it is resistance or insecurity on the architect's part that architecture needs to hold on to its relevance. Would you say the field is losing relevance?

PU   I would not say so, no. The Venice Architecture Biennale is almost as crowded as the Art Biennale. If you look at the presence of artists in the media, they almost have as much presence as movie stars or politicians.

ML   I would categorize relevance and attention as two separate domains that could take on their own trajectories. While the relevance of architecture could be diminishing, the attention that architecture is getting is increasingly inordinate. In the course of history their rise and fall often coincide, but there are specific moments when they took on opposite paths. When was the moment this fissure began to occur? Was this moment similar to the phenomenon of the eighties, when the global economy was growing and the security of architecture's cultural position led to a wide range of exegesis?

PU   Usually the Nineteenth International Congress of the International Union of Architects in Barcelona in 1996 is defined as the starting point of "star architecture." Certainly the phenomenon is prominent toward the millennium, and today the number of architecture students is still growing. This means that design has been transformed into a central activity of society and that architects, in their formation and their capacity to handle everything, seem to be at a good place at the moment. So I would say that there is a lot of influence at present.

ML   While architecture seems to be occupying a central position, I am concerned that this influence is transitory, as the means of sustaining this position are too far separated from the means of advancing the discipline. I once had a conversation with an art dealer who commented on the amount of transactions that take place during the Venice Biennale's art exhibition. By contrast, there are no transactions during the architecture exhibition that have an impact on the market, even as they are well attended—particularly by academics and writers. Nobody is there to select an architect to build a house, whereas, at art biennales, there is a lot of engagement with the marketplace. In the American architectural context, this detachment is very apparent. The people who are creating influence are not directly engaged in the field of practice. When I came to ETH Zurich [Swiss Federal Institute of Technology] in the nineteen-nineties, I was struck by academia's direct engagement with practice. If you are a professor at ETH the general public considers you to be knowledgeable and capable of building. In the United States, it is almost the opposite. You often have to go out of your way to prove that you can engage in practice despite being involved in academia. So the architectural culture in the United States, which primarily resides in academia, is an orbital structure in its relation to the profession.

PU   That is perhaps a function of the different ways the building industry is organized. You could not really imagine John Portman teaching at UCLA. And it is still somewhat considered a sin if Peter Eisenman actually builds. You know very well that by building you become suspicious. In continental Europe, the situation is quite down-to-earth. You can read about architects in the newspaper; they are around and part of reality. The situation in the United States is certainly much more raw. There is no welfare state protecting architects from the pressure of investment. The struggle for profit and the recklessness of competition is obvious. Your projects all seem to be aware of this pressure. They make clear that their environment is potentially dangerous.

ML   I never thought about it consciously, but I think there is always an interest on our part in being inside a room, but not in the center of that room. This refers not so much to the projects but rather to our position within a larger discourse. I think having been closely involved in academia the last fifteen years and being surrounded by colleagues with a dominant predilection for digital design, we are interested in a position that is not isolated or esoteric but tends to be slightly off-center. This was a protective mechanism we subconsciously adopted for ourselves. We try to obtain an overview of what is happening but avoid being blindly driven or captured as prisoners by the flow. Metaphorically, we often feel like nomads within the architectural culture of the United States—we are there, but not there at the same time.

This text is based on conversations held in Zurich on July 13, 2011 and in Houston on September 14, 2011.

Sale House

DESIGN YEARS
2001–2002

CONSTRUCTION YEARS
2003–2004

LOCATION
Venice, California, United States

SITE AREA
362 m² / 3,900 sf

FLOOR AREA
223 m² / 2,400 sf

CLIENT
Josh Sale and Peggy Curran

PRINCIPALS
Sharon Johnston and Mark Lee

PROJECT TEAM
Lars Holt, Mark Rea Baker, David Benjamin,
Jeff Adams, Diego Arraigada, Michelle
Cintron, Daveed Kapoor, Anne Rosenberg,
Anton Schneider

STRUCTURAL ENGINEER
William Koh and Associates

CONTRACTOR
Alonzo Construction

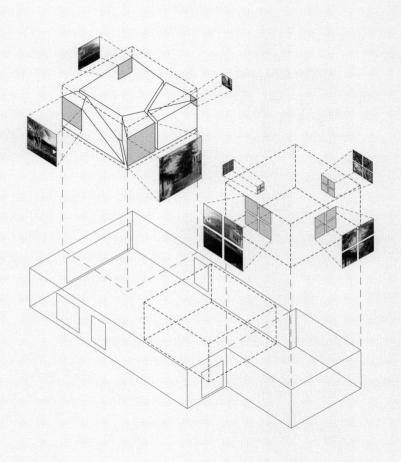

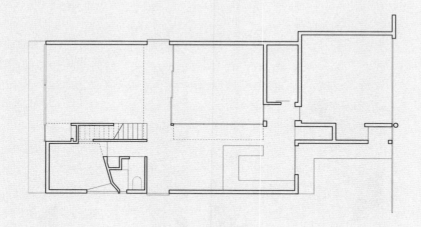

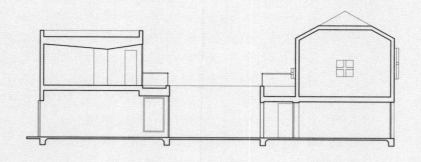

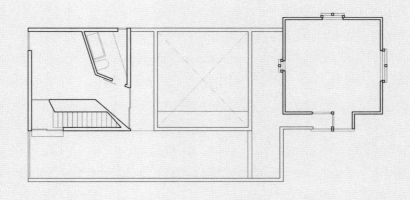

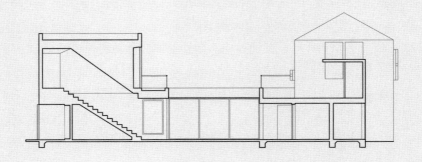

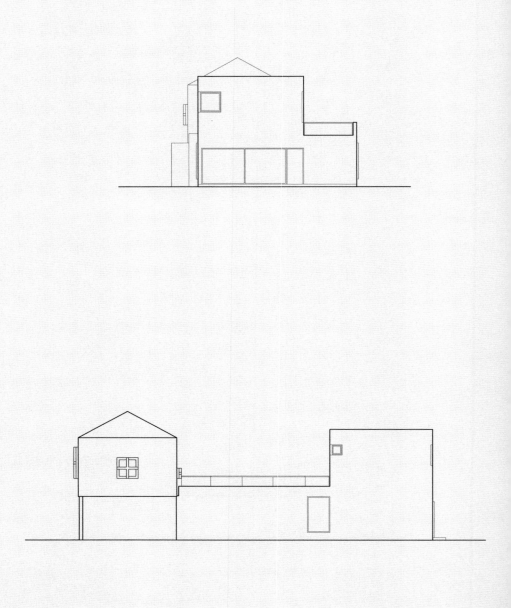

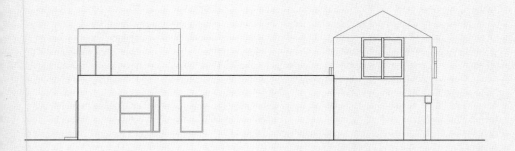

View House
Rosario
Argentina
2009

Portrait

Nicolás Valentini

II)

On Reflectivity

Sharon Johnston and Mark Lee in conversation with

Raymund Ryan

Johnston Marklee, 1787, *The Street*, Shenzen and Hong Kong Bi-City Biennale, 2011.

RR   At the 2011 Shenzhen & Hong Kong Bi-City Biennale of Urbanism/Architecture you were represented in "The Street Exhibition" alongside eleven contemporaries from Asia, Europe, and the Americas. Your installation reflected a consciousness of time, era, and history. As marked on its facade, you played with the year 1787, the year the U.S. Constitution was written. And, as suggested by Terence Riley, the exhibition's curator, you made specific reference to Paolo Portoghesi's "Strada Novissima," presented at the 1980 Venice Biennale. Four of the twelve projects that formed the temporary street in China used reflective surfaces. I am interested in reflection as a device that enlarges space. There is an interesting shift between the twenty projects in Venice in 1980 and the twelve projects in Shenzhen. In both exhibitions, there was a street and there were facades, but this recent iteration of the street project also involved thinking about space, volume, and multidimensionality.

SJ   We wanted to take on the notion of facade but also felt that there was an imperative to engage the space behind the facade with the space of the street. We saw a tension between the interiority produced by the reflective panels and the street. If the historic "Strada" focused on the collective continuity of the street and the primacy of the differentiated facade, we saw our project as an opportunity to merge the space of the interior with the autonomy of the street facade. The curved, reflective interior surface duplicates the street elevation to envelop the entire space in a panoramic room.

ML   There is indeed an abundance of reflectivity used for illusionistic purposes in "The Street Exhibition." In Alejandro Aravena's installation, for example, the facade was deliberately set back from the street such that the flanking mirrored sidewalls would extend it to infinitum and simulate a larger housing project. For us, by contrast, reflectivity is used less for illusionistic purposes than as a spatial device for duplication. I am thinking of Adolf Loos or Ludwig Mies van der Rohe and their use of materials with various degrees of reflectivity. Whether the reflectivity appears on glass, on the mirror-plated columns, on the reflecting pool, on the onyx, or on the marble, there is always an effect of duplication. We are interested in duplication not as a means for spatial expansion but rather as a means for spatial introspection. We are intrigued by the sense of complete immersion, like an infinity loop, enabled by the facade acting as a firewall that isolates the interior from the street itself.

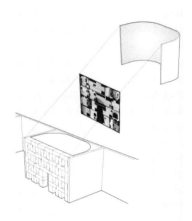

Johnston Marklee, 1787, *The Street*, Shenzen and Hong Kong Bi-City Biennale, 2011, interior.

Ludwig Mies van der Rohe, Barcelona Pavilion, 1928.

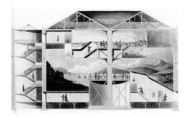

RR I had not realized that the year 1787 also saw the invention of both Potemkin's Village and Robert Barker's panorama. The idea of making reference to the invention of the panorama is intriguing and appropriate because much of your work is about forms of viewing and how apertures affect space.

Robert Mitchell, Robert Barker's panorama at Leicester Square, London, 1793, aquatint.

ML For us, panorama is a totally immersive, self-reflective atmosphere. It is an extreme version of what we have been interested in: the dual roles of building apertures, of simultaneously looking out and looking in, or of making one more aware of the interior space from where one is looking out. This coexistence of spatial expansion and immersion is an effect we have been trying to achieve both through the use of apertures and the massing of buildings. In the Porch House, for example, the large glass wall responds to the expansive view of the background and the slightly curved massing of the building responds to the slight curvature of the valley in the middle ground to create a counterpoint to the flat glass wall. But, more importantly, the curvature of the building creates a degree of self-reflectivity; it looks back at itself while looking out at the same time. It establishes a latent focal point in the middle ground: a midpoint between the curved soffits of the interior and the horizon line in the distance.

Johnston Marklee, Porch House, Los Angeles, 2013.

SJ We conceived of the installation in Shenzhen and the panorama as a kind of total aperture. It is only interrupted by deliberate rectilinear openings and gaps in the concrete street facade that open into the space of the collective exhibition and the street. The rare glimpse out interrupts the immersive atmosphere of the panorama such that the spatial experience oscillates between totality and flatness. The Sale House was probably the first direct study of this problem: the aperture is the room and the room is the aperture.

Johnston Marklee, Sale House, Los Angeles, 2004.

THICKNESS AND WEIGHT

RR Your installation in Shenzhen also represents a paradox that is present in much of your work. On the one hand you create buildings that are stable and feel protected, maybe even cave-like; on the other hand they are white and clean, balanced as volumes, and open up to incredible views. I am thinking specifically of the Hill House.

SJ By focusing on how windows could be absorbed into larger apertures, such as negative volumes, we transform the logic of a structural diagram. And we reshaped the building mass and structure in relation to the apertures, rather than simply cutting an opening in the plane of the facade. This development inspired our examination of thickness and weight, depth and profile in contrast to a more conventional approach to building envelopes, skins, frames, and articulated material assemblies. We have never done a project about frames and framing as a device to make space. It has always rather been about carving to form an aperture. In the Hill House we resolved the contrasting demands for heaviness, mass, and structure on the hill with the desire for volume, large openings, and a view. These contrasting conditions produce a dynamic equilibrium of space and structure.

Johnston Marklee, Hill House, Los Angeles, 2004.

Johnston Marklee, En Sully, Switzerland, 2010.

Alvar Aalto, Säynätsalo Town Hall, Finland, 1949–52.

RR When I saw your residential proposal for Switzerland, En Sully, I was surprised to find myself thinking of Aalto. I thought of his Säynätsalo Town Hall, a building in the middle of a small town with forest around it, a building with a pure interior space that seeps to the outside. Your Swiss project in particular has this kind of feeling. Of course the apartments and the houses will all be worked out but, more critically, you give people a bigger shared space. That principle could become a much bigger project—whether in the middle of a town or in a developing ex-urban context. You establish a legible, communal space that becomes the main space, the pure space of the project. So, in that case, at least the way I read it, the functional space, the set of rooms the client probably requested, are, in fact, poché.

ML We started off with the largest possible figure, something thick and dense and then started carving out a series of interlocked courtyards. The resulting courtyards create an intermediate scale of public space that is more defined and enclosed than the more expansive outdoor spaces surrounding the building. At the end the project oscillates between appearing as a single building and a series of buildings agglomerated together. The courtyards are intimate in the same way that medieval villages might seem to be, metaphysical in the sense that they are self-referential and yet specifically connected to their place, not unlike the courtyard at the Säynätsalo Town Hall.

SJ We also thought about the house as an inversion—an inside out project—because the transparency, openness, and flexibility you are interpreting as kind of poché are on the outside and the thick, carved zones are within the block.

ML You referred to an approach in which a subdued exterior conceals a more perverse and exuberant interior. This approach also stems from Loos, who often maintained a gentlemanly disposition for the exterior of his buildings that

108

allowed him to be, by contrast, very hedonistic or indulgent in the interior. This kind of opposition is an ideal analogy for the relationship between architecture and the city today. There is a collective decorum that provides cohesion and allows, thereby, for idiosyncrasy and individualism on a smaller scale.

Johnston Marklee, Grand Traiano Art Complex, Grottaferrata, Italy, 2008.

RR   You achieved this early on in the Sale House. And in more recent projects—at least in the models—the Gran Traiano complex in Grottaferrata, Italy, mirrors the idea of a cool exterior with a hot interior.

ML   One might think of cool as also dumb. Dumb both in terms of volume as well as in terms of intellect. It is not only a matter of politeness or decorum in relationship to the building and the city, but it's also related to a particular Los Angeles ethos of coolness, one that promotes a detachment as well as a delay of engagement.

Kazuo Shinohara, House in White, Suginami, Tokyo, Japan, 1966.

RR   I was recently in Japan and had the chance to see some of Kazuo Shinohara's work. It is incredibly provocative and moving, and it touches you in unexpected ways. I was intrigued by his ability to relate to a larger architectural culture. His early projects were, at first glance, like traditional Japanese houses. They allowed him to create interiors both stunningly Modernist and oddly sensuous. This relates to your work in the sense that it is, like Shinohara's, about carving. While Los Angeles architecture is hardly about carving, that kind of form has a strong presence in your projects, both in section and in plan. This inevitably brings up poché, something I seldom think about when considering Los Angeles, where everything seems to just hang out, to be clipped on or applied. By contrast, much of your work is clever in a way I would describe as serving space. I mean this not necessarily in purely mechanical terms, nor as with Kahn's "served" and "servant" spaces. In your projects there is often a large space, a void or an aperture, that exists just for space's sake.

ML   Indeed. A project such as the Vault House was conceived as a series of rooms carved or hollowed out of a solid. The fundamental separation of interior from exterior forms relieves the relational constraints between the singular exterior volume and the multiple interior volumes. The resulted poché thus enabled us to conceal the structural and mechanical clumsiness that is typical of American construction. But I would emphasize that the notion of carving or subtraction stems from a spatial and conceptual perspective rather than one pertaining to construction; the form of the vault does not signify the primacy of stereotomic over tectonic approaches to construction.

sj In the View House, we first designed the exterior envelope according to zoning criteria and the logics of cast-in-place concrete and then organized the interior. The design stitches together interior space and exterior envelope through the logic of apertures, the cuts and slices in the overall mass, and the resulting building structure. The View House is the first project in which we became interested in this space between the exterior facade and the interior enclosure, and in which we began to contour these spaces very consciously. For example at night, in the living room, the butt joint glass corner dissolves visually. A space emerges that, like a soap bubble, is neither interior nor exterior but rather a mediating threshold. House House at Ordos is another example of our interest in these in-between spaces through the question of aperture. Our approach to flatness and depth, volume and solid mass seen through the development of the openings, patios, and vertical light cores affects the ambiguity of how one perceives lightness, flatness, heaviness, and depth in the design of a house.

ml But it is not as one directional as it seems; it's not just about carving. Once we carve to the bone then something protrudes again. The issue you brought up indirectly relates to mass and weight. When we present the Vault House to our European or Latin American colleagues, for example, they are sometimes shocked that it is a steel frame structure rather than a stereotomic construction process, like concrete or masonry. But beyond the tectonic ontology there is also the very pragmatic issue of the physical weight of the building. The house is built on the beach, on sand, so making it as light as possible was a requirement. Cross bracing was essential to allow all of the mechanical spaces to go through the poché space. We were not interested in building a massive structure. Instead, we aimed to create a building that, like a kite, would convey lightness in terms of weight but not in terms of appearance. Of course, this is also a way of addressing this level of construction and ambition with the type of budget available in Los Angeles. We could never approach this like Kazuyo Sejima or Herzog & de Meuron would. It would be an uphill battle. We have to think of a way to build within our specific economic and cultural context.

sj We accept how one has to build within the American construction system. It is essential to take on that challenge and learn to use it as a constraint that can perform.

rr This reminds me of architects like Alvaro Siza or Eduardo Souto de Moura, who are very conscious of what they can

Johnston Marklee, Vault House, Oxnard, California, 2013, construction photo.

Johnston Marklee, Vault House, Oxnard, California, 2013.

110

and cannot do in terms of local craft and the peculiarities of regional building industries. At this point Siza must have excellent relations with contractors in Portugal. Souto de Moura, I believe, refuses to build far away for precisely this reason. They are able to proceed slowly, in dialog with tradespeople and other colleagues.

ML   Context is important for us. Here I not only mean the physical context but also the cultural context, as well as the context of construction to which you refer. More importantly, in today's global practices the notion of the local is different. What differentiates two separate contexts has less to do with the latitude in which they reside than with the building laws to which they are subject. Instead of building styles, the rules that dictate building parameters such as maximum density, height, volume, insulation, fire safety, and construction methods constitute the context to which the architect responds. In that sense, people that we admire, who are not necessarily stylistically alike, like Siza or even Gehry, understand this notion of context very well.

RR   I find that people still don't give Gehry sufficient credit for his persistent interest in how things get built and how to get each project through the system. That goes from using 2×4s and chain link to using contemporary computer technologies. This, of course, is a sense of context not simply as aesthetics and massing but as economy and local expertise.

MONTAGE

RR   Let's talk about the art world. You've been tracking the art world since you were students. In all of your work you seem to be tapping into a notion of the view. And that's the view whether it's a framed view of nature or the photographic view of the panorama. How has working with artists influenced your thinking about the role of the image and the appeal, perhaps, of some ideal image? Hill House and at least one half of the project for Chile suggest the idea of the *mirador* looking across the landscape. If you are surrounded by open fields or mountains or the ocean, strategies like that can work very well. But what about in less bucolic settings? Has art practice informed your approach in such cases?

ML   Contemporary art practices have certainly influenced our work, from afar and from up close. But I would say it's more that they have affected our way of thinking and looking at things from an oblique perspective than that they provide mechanisms with which to address the notion of the view. We do not claim to be art historians and find the type of work that professes to address critical notions of the view unbecoming. Nevertheless, the visual sensibility of art practices has seeped into the representations of our work, especially from photography, from Jan Dibbets and Dan Graham to Olafur Eliasson

111

and Cyprien Gaillard, in all of whose work the dynamics between the frame of the picture and the horizon line within the
picture forms an incredible tension. Having designed projects
in many such bucolic landscapes we became interested in the
notion that the building act not only as an apparatus to view
landscape, such as is the case with the Lee Pollak House,
for example, but also that it become a doppelganger of the
landscape, such as at the Chile House. Naturally, this interest
in doubling the landscape progressed to the panorama.

Johnston Marklee, Chile House, Penco, Chile,
2011.

RR With regard to the panorama or the grand view, and
thinking about some of our favorite Modernist architects, the
images we are frequently drawn to are not necessarily factual
photographs but, as in the case of Mies, collages and pho-
tomontages. There is something about capturing the essence
of an idea through the constructed image. Do you agree that
montage is both a tactic for you as designers and a means for
the client to get to the spirit of a project?

ML Our use of collages and collaboration with artists started
with Julius Shulman. When we were designing the Hill House
we made a collage with Shulman's 1960 photograph of Case
Study House #22, designed by Pierre Koenig, who was a
teacher of mine. In our collage we took away the cantilevered
roof, the floor slab, the foreground in Shulman's image—like
Robert Rauschenberg erasing de Kooning's drawing—and
distilled this well-known image, which remains such an emblem
of postwar living in Southern California, to its raw elements:
an open architectural corner projecting out toward a distant
view. The result of this collage allowed us to understand the
significance of continuing the profile of the house, uninter-
rupted by any windows or apertures. When Shulman saw what
we did to his image he came to the finished house and took a
series of photographs of it. It was a very interesting moment in
the cycle of creative processes: his photograph was a source
for the design of the house and the finished house in turn

Johnston Marklee, Hill House, Los Angeles,
2004, photograph by Julius Shulman.

became a source for his new photographs, like a feedback loop of sorts. Seeing how Shulman's new photographs took on a life of their own, we began to invite artists to photograph our buildings, not in the typical way of architectural photography, in which the building is the main subject matter, but rather such that the building plays a role in each artist's own narrative. We were thrilled to see how unanticipated narratives began to emerge from the projects.

Pierre Koenig, Case Study House #22 (Stahl House), Los Angeles, 1959, photograph by Julius Shulman.

Johnston Marklee, Hill House, Los Angeles, collage with Case Study House #22, 2004.

TRANSCENDING SCALES

RR   You previously mentioned House House, which, as its name implies, has also to do with doubleness. Rather than building another single house in the context of the other ninety-nine houses for Ordos, you proposed a building that would offer a somewhat mutant quality: a house and a half. Your project is not the typical double house; it is, rather, one and a half houses, an idea I like very much as it signals beyond the individual family house on its lot to a kind of collectivity. This is, of course, a bugbear for nearly every Los Angeles architect: how to go from making a house, no matter how beautiful and elegant, to something with a larger urban social role and suggestiveness.

ML   This is something that we are facing right now. We currently have opportunities that are larger in scale than typical for us. And we are very well aware of architects who have not managed to translate their work to new scales as well as others might have. The question at hand is if we want to adapt to larger, scaleless incarnations of what we have done before or if an aggregation of elements becomes inevitable. This is something we realized when working on the UCLA Graduate Studios and on the Menil Drawing Institute in Houston. While in smaller-scaled projects, we start with singular objects, then begin doubling them, and then further multiply them into agglomerations, these larger projects require a new singularity. When we reach a certain size project, as we have now, a new scale needs to be introduced to unify the smaller parts. In the cases of UCLA and the Menil, the singular roof is introduced to provide coherence for the projects.

Johnston Marklee, Menil Drawing Institute, Houston, 2012–17.

RR In the charrette to extend New York's MoMA in the late 1990s, Herzog & de Meuron differentiated between an "Agglomerate Type," with separate buildings somewhat like objects in a still life, as with certain postmodern assemblages, and a "Conglomerate Type," with a consistent datum for facade and roof through which special elements might occasionally protrude. I take it that your attitude to larger projects falls more in the "Conglomerate" camp. Other architects, architects as different from one another as are Bernard Tschumi and Renzo Piano, have utilized the unifying potential of The Big Roof. In your case, however, the roof is not simply a unilateral canopy. You are interested in the potential to carve spaces or voids within a larger mass, spaces no longer at a residential but rather at an institutional or even urban scale.

ML This difference between an Agglomerate versus a Conglomerate Type translates to adopting an additive versus a subtractive approach to design, similar to the way Valerio Olgiati divided the world of architects into those who add and those who subtract. While we generally use subtractive approaches for smaller projects like houses and additive approaches for larger projects such as institutions they are ultimately only the means to find the right scale for the building. Aldo van Eyck had written about the notion of "the right size" in buildings. The right scale, however, is something more relational to the building's context and more dynamic. For us, the right scale typically hovers between the perfect scale of harmonious equilibrium and a scale that is slightly off, slightly awkward, slightly too big or too small. The first one is static, the second dynamic. I.M. Pei and Richard Meier master the state of harmonious equilibrium, which most people strive for and which architects like. It's not an easy feat. Being off scale and doing it right is also very hard; it can come across as contrived very easily. But to hover between the harmonious and the off scale is the hardest. And the difference between a small and a larger-scaled project is that the margin of fluctuation between a static and dynamic state is smaller in a house-scaled project of a private nature and greater in an institutionally scaled project of a public nature.

INTERNATIONALISM

RR   You've built up a practice doing houses, stores, and installation work in Los Angeles. Very quickly, however, you have also had the opportunity to take on projects in Argentina, Italy, Switzerland, and Chile. How do you account for this splendid success? What do you see as the differences and the advantages in building away from home?

sj   The breadth of our projects is partially due to circumstance and can, in part, also be attributed to our connection to the art world. One of the things we realized early on is that we had to leave the United States to find opportunities for larger projects before we could come home to do projects of a similar scale here in America. I don't think it's just an issue in Los Angeles; I think it's probably an American issue. The United States is a risk-averse place and we felt we had to leave before we could come back and get things done here.
ml   From a professional standpoint it is clear that if we stayed in the United States and we hadn't done ten libraries, we wouldn't have been able to build a single one. So we had to go out of our way to find opportunities to test and try things that we couldn't otherwise.

RR   I wonder if the apparent ease in taking on foreign projects isn't at least in part due to a generational consciousness. Might there be advantages to letting professional ego go to one side and relaxing a bit—you know, the hackneyed old myth of the Starchitect? Is it fair to detect this in the way you work with colleagues abroad, an openness to see what opportunities might lie in collaboration?

sj   The structure of this book is a reflection of our approach to collaboration. We plan for partnerships, seek out ways to productively pass the baton back and forth, so to speak. And we probably find our collaborators as much as they find us. We take part in a discourse already in place between a loose group of architects. And many of the overseas projects are initiated by other architects, arising as opportunities for multiple architects or a collection of projects. We share a common set of interests and our collected work explores related themes through the variable lens of each individual office. In addition, we are much more involved with some of our clients—like in the case of Pierpaolo Barzan, the founder of the Depart Foundation—beyond the architectural project. We also work on installations, books, public events, et cetera. So it becomes a much deeper dialog and exchange.

Sharon Johnston, Ordos, Inner Mongolia, January 2008.

ml   It is also a way for us to constantly refresh ourselves. I think that wherever someone is, there is always something

Oedipal, something about reacting to the generation before. The generation before us had this demiurgic posture of architecture, they understood themselves as the ones who would save the world and we eventually realized that they would not. So I think this reflection always keeps us fresh. We also look to collaboration as a means to unhinge what we know. We see artists as coconspirators and, because we don't have a vested interest in their world, it allows us to be very free in terms of exchange. Unlike architecture, which is often constrained by its politics, art allows for what we see as a kind of freshness.

RR   And this allows you to invent a new language or code of conduct?

ML   There is a certain directness about artists' ways of working that makes us feel liberated.

RR   Though, wouldn't you agree, successful artists also have to position their work in particular ways to get to the essence of what they are trying to say?

SJ   In contrast to certain trends in architecture, in which the boundaries are becoming more and more blurred, Mark and I are interested in working at the core of the discipline. But we like to work with artists and experts in other disciplines in a way that is not about being an artist or emulating another discipline but more about exchange or the transposition of ideas and practices. For example we designed the show Later Layer, at the Italian Cultural Institute in Los Angeles, together with Walead Beshty. The collaboration included the design of the exhibition and a series of objects that were born out of our common interest in seriality and notions of the multiple. We were pursuing a shared set of interests with very different materials and means and it became a very fertile discussion that produced both the objects and an ongoing dialog.

Johnston Marklee with Walead Beshty, *Later Layer*, Italian Cultural Institute, Los Angeles, 2010.

RR   In the mid-nineties I was writing frequently for *Blueprint* and interviewed Jacques Herzog and Daniel Libeskind around the same time. I ended both interviews by asking about the relationship of art and architecture and if architecture was art. Herzog was emphatic that architecture is not art, whereas Libeskind stressed that architecture is art and always has been art.

ML   I think we would side more with Herzog. There is a certain interiority or autonomy about architecture and I feel that because we are secure about that autonomy, we can look into a lot of techniques of artists that could be brought into architecture and vice versa. I also want to address that question in a more profane way. There is the more altruistic way of creative exchange but I also think that working with the art world—not just artists, but also collectors, institutions, and galleries—we encounter more people who can translate cultural capital into mercantile capital. In other words, there is more funny money in the art world. In the architecture world, eighty percent is tied to real-estate value. So to elevate it from mere building to architecture you need something else and you need a type of audience that understands that.

SJ   In Europe architecture has more capital in and of its own. Banks have to invest a certain percentage of their cash in architecture, in buildings. The longevity of a building is five times what one might invest if they were building a house in America and this translates into the size and quality of resources that developers and clients are willing to invest. It's strategic to find sectors stateside, such as cultural institutions and art patrons, which recognize the cultural value of architecture.

ML   On another occasion, you referred to Aldo Rossi, his pureness of volume and, as a result, how often inhuman those volumes can be. To counter this, we always try to inject a certain imperfection into the project.

BEAUTY IN IMPERFECTION AND DISTORTION

RR   Which is like many great artworks.

ML   Oftentimes it is this imperfection that draws people in. It is an imperfection that creates a familiarity, or is a prelude to something unfamiliar, metaphysical, or exceptional; we are looking at qualities that ultimately separate mere building from architecture.

RR   There are affinities, in such tactics of imperfection, to some of David Hockney's work: once, when young and impoverished, he incorporated a small rip in the paper by illustrating an athlete stumbling across this physical blemish. In the case of Ellsworth Kelly, a very different artist, what we may at first glance think is a classic rectangle, for instance, turns out on closer inspection to be a delicate quadrilateral or other impure shape.

ML   We love Hockney, too. There was a similar example in his photo collages. In one of the pieces in the series, one of the rows was overexposed at the one-hour photo-processor and the clerk wrote him an apologetic letter. He eventually put that letter on top of the corner of the area where that photograph was missing.

RR   That relates to Louis Pasteur's phrase, that chance favors the prepared mind. Gehry is often able to capitalize on quirks of the site or what happens during the construction process. I am thinking of how he incorporated the nineteen-thirties dairy at the Edgemar complex, of how various tilted windows offered edited views of foliage and sky as at his own home, and of the way he exposes 2×4s and other building components

Frank Gehry, Edgemar Development, Santa
Monica, California, 1984.

almost as ornament. In the case of the Fish and Snake lamps in the eighties, he apparently got the idea for the scale-like skin when a piece of laminate smashed by accident.

ML   We think Gehry is a master at this. The way he injects imperfection into his projects conveys humanity and ultimately imbues his projects with a generosity that many architects who followed his path could never replicate.

SJ   In the View House the view out into the landscape is important, but there is also a complex inner landscape where oblique views are doubled, paired, and masked out. It's as much about masking things out as it is about seeing through to something else. The pairing or simultaneity of views is not necessarily oppositional; these spaces have an imperfection, a denial of something perfect to offer something more complex, something with more range and duration.

RR   Because you are not building temples to calcified belief systems, whether religion or money.

SJ   In the Chile House project, you go through this processional path or promenade and then there's the view and there is something very subversive about this sort of dull reflected doubling of that view behind you. It's not quite as serene, and you need to turn around and look back. You need to think and keep moving. The experience is not about the stationary view, and you need to recall where you were before.

ML   And this motion is what gives it a vernacular dimension.

RR   For a long time beauty was a kind of no-no. Your work is informed by theory, but it also evokes beauty. Clients may assume beauty as a starting point, whereas many serious architects shy away from beauty, as if it's not only unattainable but also somehow dirty. Dirty beauty—there's a title! Do you agree that the intent to make a beautiful thing is once again considered a worthy task, whereas twenty years ago it would have seemed questionable?

ML   The kind of beauty that we are attracted to, whether it's our project or another person's project, is a kind of beauty that borders on something else. A kind of you're not quite sure exactly is beautiful or not.

RR   Isn't this also the case with human beings, between men and women? A beautiful face, say—some imperfection in the eye or nose or mouth renders the portrait more compelling.

ML   The most intriguing type of beauty leaves you not quite sure whether, for example, a woman is very beautiful or very ugly. There is a kind of mystery about that uncertainty that prompts one to look again and probe deeper. Rather than flat out one-dimensional, what-you-see-is-what-you-get beauty, the imperfect beauty takes time to unfold and requires attention, and the more you probe into it the more it gives. So the work aims for this sort of imperfect, challenging beauty. These are not temples to be gazed at, in awe, from a stationary vantage point and, objects to which critique is bestowed from above. We feel that architecture doesn't really have the broad sociocritical power it once did. We think that the critique has to be much more subtle. That it should posit new forms that embody this unfolding, truer beauty.

This text is based on a conversation held in Shenzhen on December 9, 2011.

View House

DESIGN YEARS
2005–2006

CONSTRUCTION YEARS
2006–2009

LOCATION
Rosario, Argentina

SITE AREA
2,113 m² / 22,744 sf

FLOOR AREA
361 m² / 3,886 sf

CLIENT
Lucas Ma, Markee LLC

PRINCIPALS
Sharon Johnston, Mark Lee
for Johnston Marklee,
Diego Arraigada
for Diego Arraigada Arquitectos

PROJECT TEAM
Juliana Espósito, Jeff Adams, Pablo Gamba,
Nazarena Infance, Nadia Carassai, Anne
Rosenberg, Anton Schneider, Amalia Gonzales

STRUCTURAL ENGINEER
Estudio Garibay

CONTRACTOR
MECSA

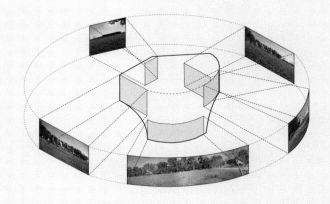

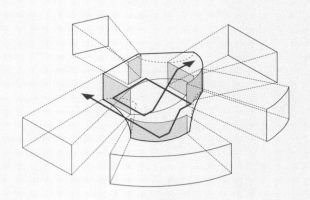

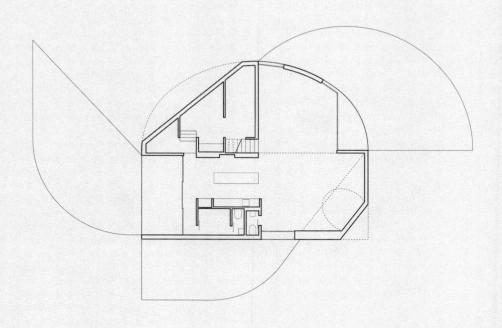

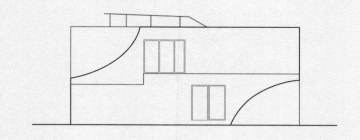

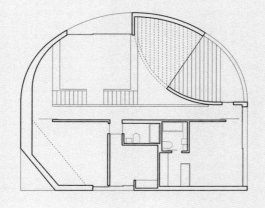

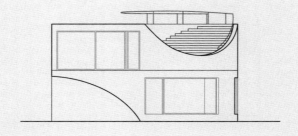

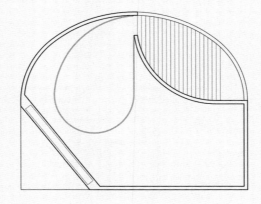

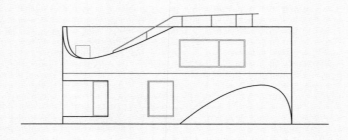

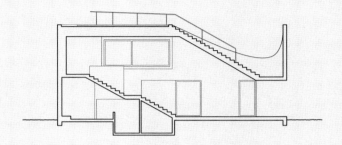

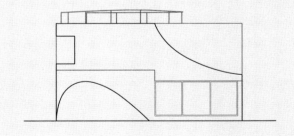

insert:

Luisa Lambri
Untitled
(Hill House)

III)

On Gravity

Sharon Johnston and Mark Lee in conversation with

Sarah Whiting

ML We receive recurring criticism from critics who would prefer us to adopt a more extreme position. For us, the middle is not an average or common denominator but rather something that embraces the tension between opposites. I know you've discussed this notion of the middle before; what do you think about the middle ground?

Ludwig Mies van der Rohe, IIT Campus, Chicago, 1947.

OMA, Casa da Musica, Porto, 2005.

SW I've taken an interest in the middle recently, though it's a hard flag to wave, of course, a hard topic to champion. The middle is associated with milque toast: with equivocation, with a little of this and a little of that. I've always been an advocate of strong agendas and strong opinions. Strong doesn't mean extreme—it means forceful enough to move forward.

And yet, I find myself right in the middle: I'm living in the middle of the country. I'm right at middle age. As a dean, I'm in the middle between administration and faculty. More importantly for this conversation, however, I see a middle ground of sorts emerging within architecture, and that's precisely why I'm interested in JML's work right now. This middle is not about size or scale, but about *strategy*. This middle is not an average, but rather a strategic oscillation that forges a new direction by capitalizing on the best of *this* as well as the best of *that*. Successful middle projects are big *and* small. They are singular but not self-sufficient; they are at once autonomous *and* engaged. They have a biased diversity, and that bias produces a gravitational intensity while simultaneously reaching beyond itself.

I first realized the promise of the middle, of projects that oscillate between two states, when writing about the superblock planning of Chicago's near South Side during the nineteen-forties: projects for IIT (Mies van der Rohe), Michael Reese Hospital (Walter Gropius, among others), Lake Meadows (SOM), Prairie Courts (Keck and Keck) that, together, created an entire district of autonomous campuses that were nevertheless interconnected by a tartan plaid plan that produced a superblock city. And while "superblock" implies enormous scale, these projects actually introduced a medium-sized urban scale—neither the smallness of the neighborhood, nor the enormity of the entire city—to Chicago.

A similar middle-like coincidence of autonomy and interconnectedness is emerging within architecture through a series of projects that embrace objecthood while simultaneously connecting to their surrounding contexts. These architectural objects are singular but not idealized—they are not complete within themselves. OMA's Casa da Musica in Porto is a good example of this kind of almost-complete singularity. It is hard to capture the building in your mind as a whole and while it is not contextual in any normative way, it clearly responds to and creates its site. The project is slightly ungainly;

it is chunky, stubby, and also strangely elegant. Several JML projects have this same quality of *engaged autonomy*—particularly the house in Rosario, which is a middle project but not a middling one. That is, it's contextual and yet singular; Rosario is a strong statement, not a murmur.

Johnston Marklee, View House, Rosario, Argentina, 2009.

ML　We've observed something in the built world that finds an apt and useful parallel in the fashion industry. I'm referring specifically to the increasing obsolescence and disconnection of haute couture from "reality." Rarified couture collections were once the spectacles from which all else trickled down, an image intended to sell the brand's perfume and ready-to-wear apparel. Eventually people realized that just because they wear a Dior fragrance doesn't mean they are at all connected to what is embodied by the brand's couture. In reaction to this consumer epiphany, fashion start-ups today seem to be aggressively colonizing the middle. They'll do an exclusive line, a diffusion line, a jeans line, together with a website and a brick-and-mortar shop. They do it all at the same time.

This development is important and reflects a parallel phenomenon within architectural culture. If one surveys what is being built in the world today, it comes down to one percent iconic buildings and the remaining 99 percent crap. Architectural discourse focuses solely on pushing the envelope represented by this one percent of exceptional, couture buildings, with the naive hope that these developments will trickle down. But instead, in actuality, it pushes the exceptional further and further away from the quotidian. The everyday rarely benefits from, let alone seeks to emulate, the experiments of the exceptional. If this trajectory continues, architecture will be more and more disconnected from the built world and, eventually, will lose its fundamental foundation as a medium worthy of discussion. So we think architecture should colonize the middle ground in a strong way and that it is the territory that most fundamentally requires excellence in response. This middle is not a distilled, generic zone. In our design process, we generally try not to distill things, but rather to consider the many factors of each project—and even add things—to maintain complexity. We're interested in pursuing the distinction between what's perceived as complexity "up front" and something more latent.

ARTICULATING THE MIDDLE

sw　Let's pause to take up that question of complexity: for me, one of the most interesting common denominators of your projects is that they eschew complexity. They have a lot going on. They are neither minimal nor "one-liners," but there always

Chris Burden, *Metropolis II*, Los Angeles County Museum of Art, 2012.

seems to be a comfortable resolution. It is like when we saw Chris Burden's fantastic installation *Metropolis II* at LACMA: what interested us in that project was that while a certain amount of "stuff going on" tends to produce utter cacophony, *Metropolis II* possessed a busy yet strangely unrestrictive visual coherence. That kind of productive coherence is the oscillation I was talking about—it's a feature that I find in your work.

ML   In a way it is complexity without contradiction.

SW   Yes, but I wouldn't even use the term complexity. For one, it necessarily evokes Robert Venturi, who isn't, for me, a relevant reference for your work. Instead of "complex," I'd say, "manifold." Maybe I am biased against "complexity," which already has so much difficulty built into it and its many syllables. Manifold rolls off your tongue; its lovely sound is equivalent to its idea. It's not difficult and it doesn't flaunt difficulty.

ML   Coming up with a surreptitious way to imply this manifold quality is of interest to us. We are attracted to projects in which the degree of difficulty inherent to the creative process is not in direct proportion to how the work is received. The conception or the making of the work may be complex and difficult, but the reception does not have to pronounce this difficulty in any explicit way.

Johnston Marklee, Vault House, Oxnard, California, 2013.

SW   Indeed—that's the key. Your work is neither simple nor complex. You can have a lot going on without demanding a painful experience to decode it. That ambition goes hand in hand with the level of beauty in your projects, which is similarly complex but immediate. Maybe that's where there is a Venturi parallel: not stylistically but rather in the both/and that the middle produces.

For me, the View House and the Vault House are just on the border of being ugly—or at least ungainly. They somehow manage to flirt with that border while remaining beautiful objects. They are somewhat indecipherable but not alien. And I think that beauty, and even ugliness, are topics rarely broached in architecture today.

ML   While we certainly don't shy away from conventional notions of beauty, we also don't feel ourselves enslaved by them. The beauty to which we are most drawn embodies certain qualities of ambiguity and foreignness. We find the beauty that unfolds over time, the type that seems ugly at first glance, much more compelling than beauty that affirms perfection and mastery at the outset. We recognize the importance of maintaining a high degree of cohesiveness in order to hold together these qualities of defamiliarization or imperfection. And, as a result of this desire for cohesion, we are sometimes labeled as minimalists.

sj   Our process of distilling works through the phases of design is not a reductive effort to minimize but rather an attempt to precisely bring conditions of space, form and structure into contact with one another. And we select just the elements we need to achieve these results. While a first look might suggest a uniform singularity, we are always much more interested in delayed discovery whereby the complexity of variations and relationships comes into focus over time.

ml   We think that when there is a repetition, when one thing does two things, we are happy, and that when one thing does three things we are even happier.

OMA, Les Halles, Paris, 2003.

sw   What's amazing is that you succeed at offering more and more, without making it difficult to get there. It goes back to the idea of the middle's objecthood having certain almost adolescent qualities of stubbiness (and maybe even an adolescent *stubbornness* that keeps everything as direct as possible). Ever since OMA produced their Les Halles scheme with stubby towers that barely exceeded the typical Parisian apartment block's six-story height, I've been interested in the "stubby." Those towers at Les Halles are not really towers—they are not elegant, elongated edifices—but they are nevertheless legible as towers. They are autonomous in that you read each one as singular, but because they are really not that big, they are also all co dependent. They produce an entirely new category between the autonomous and the contextual or the group. It's the same with the so-called "chunky" in your work. *Chunky*, which is how Ron [Witte] characterized your work when you lectured at Rice University, is a word I also find fairly distasteful on certain levels. If we talk about how words sound, it's simply an ugly sounding word. At the same time, *chunky* has substance to it. Maybe the chunky is where the ungainly object has not yet reached its perfect state, but is instead in a gawky and transitional moment. Maybe it describes things that possess the possibility of becoming elegant but aren't there yet. The middle gets exciting when it's understood as being in this adolescent stage, rather than as a stage of compromise, lack, or just *non* (the *not-this*, the *not-that*). In other words, rather than seeing the middle as a way of avoiding a statement, it can be a very nuanced statement unto itself. Your work, which lets the middle emerge as a category of its own, breaks this middle as "not," middle as avoidance, middle as compromise. It makes something of the middle.

ml   This is something that preoccupies us too. We are convinced that the middle should not simply be the static average or equilibrium between two worlds, but should rather be a dynamic oscillation between the high and the low and the big and the small. The threshold between medium and big and medium and small is a charged space. When you use the term chunkiness, or terms like slumping, there is an aspect of implied failure that we like. It's related to the way we prefer the effect of "levitating" to the more deterministic "cantilevering." Levitation suggests weight and buoyancy rather than the heroic constructivist impulses of the anti-gravitational. Levitation implies an interesting equilibrium that is dynamic rather than homeostatic.

SJ   In contrast to explicitly heroic aspirations we are interested in awkwardness, which becomes apparent as your experience of a space moves in and out of balance, assumes one quality and then another. We are interested in architecture that is not fully formed or that is continually reforming, in imperfect spaces and forms, in almost ugly things. For example in the View House, some of the cuts into the mass impart a sensation of slumping and embedment into the ground. Alternatively, spherical slices result in lofted moments in which the house appears to spring out of the ground. We like to introduce these contradictory conditions within one project by means of deviating repetitions of simple operations.

ML   For us, this interest in the middle might have stemmed from a reaction to the generation before us, a generation of self-proclaimed rebels who eventually became the establishment. They were all about provocation and choosing sides, about radicalism without a sense of measure, about pushing the envelope at all cost, rather than the quality of the architecture or its execution.

SJ   This effort to define the middle is not about avoiding but rather about intensifying contrasts of scale and form. Our focus on edges versus surface, and the muteness of our assemblies and building systems, has allowed us to intensify spatial relationships and conditions of viewing that would otherwise be lost in a field of over-articulated "intricacy." With the aspects of blankness that many of our interiors have, and with the conventional details of frames, trims and depth often missing, one can discover a new middle register. We suggest an oscillating space between the immediate, abstract foreground of a particular room, material, or silhouette, and the more distant view captured through apertures or between spaces.

ML   To succeed in the middle, one needs to have control. We aspire to have the type of design control in which the result is generous. When considering works that are arguably "sparse," the ones that stand out are works that are sparse but also somehow very generous. If you look at Alvaro Siza's work or Alvar Aalto's work, the spaces could be sparse, but you can put a Victorian chair in them and they still work. By contrast, there are austere spaces that are imposing, spaces

GENEROSITY

that can only be furnished with Barcelona chairs that line up, or else something feels out of balance. We find this type of work rather suffocating and ungenerous. We are fighting for control in certain aspects of our own work so that liberation can happen somewhere else later.

Alvar Aalto, Villa Mairea, Noormarkku, Finland, 1939.

sw Generosity is a perfect term. It suggests a controlled form of exaggeration: polite or considerate excess that has a certain grace to it. Your point about control and liberation is for me the quintessential OMA project—it's what Rem's always pursued: how do you set up parameters that, paradoxically, produce freedom? All too often architects seem to think that this combination of control and liberation necessitates a shock mechanism or a radical juxtaposition in which, say, your world is turned upside down in order to give you freedoms you wouldn't anticipate. The best OMA projects are those in which the volume of that shock value is turned way, way low. As in Porto, for example. In Johnston Marklee's work, the freedoms are often of a gentler nature. Your projects ease into freedom almost without realizing it. It's part of your control. There's an enormous amount of control in your work, but it is a seemingly effortless control that generates architectural *generosity*, which, yes, is the perfect term.

ML We are certainly not after a sadomasochistic type of control! For us, the notion of liberation is not necessarily dictated by the architect, but by the beholder or occupier who is enabled by the conditions provided by the architecture. Sometimes it is as simple as making the roof or ceiling as strong as possible so that it can absorb a lot of mess underneath it. Not everything underneath the roof consequently needs to be organized in a grid, but the constraints and coherence offered by the roof provide freedom to the rest of the project.

Johnston Marklee, Poggio Golo Winery, Tuscany, Italy, 2008.

sj These notions of control and generosity are linked to how we establish and value logics of coherence in our work. Part of how we collect, assimilate, and articulate knowledge and design attributes is through a bottom up collation of individual and collective systems. The strong continuous curvature of the roof in the Poggio Golo winery, for example, provides weight and gravity to the form, allowing us to carve out voids, pockets, and apertures, while the overall figure of the tripartite wings remains intact and legible.

ML I would further distinguish the act of collecting—whether it is knowledge or artifacts—from the act of mere accumulation or hoarding. Collecting necessitates discernment and deliberation. It involves establishing value systems of judgment with which to select and edit.

JUDGMENT

sw It's true that judgment distinguishes collecting or curating from accumulating or hoarding. And one develops the ability to judge through such an exercise. But before ascertaining what interests you around you, I'm interested in Johnston Marklee's architectural judgment. My ongoing obsession with the topic of judgment stems from a desire to address two big questions that are too often skirted. First: how *design judgment* happens—how decisions are made at the inception and during the development of a project—and then how *evaluative judgment* happens, how we evaluate or critique work. What are Johnston Marklee's criteria, your parameters of judgment?

ML As architects we have to be judgmental, in the sense that having a position toward one's own work as well as other's work is important. Being judgmental of other work helps us to articulate and sharpen our own values. And we try to be very specific with our judgments. At the same time, we are very private about the judgments we have established. To establish judgment is a deeply personal matter and not a means to attack or be critical of others. We have no desire to turn every issue into a trivial debate. To form judgment is a way to establish an internal value system. One is always being accused of being too much of this and not enough of that and others will inevitably attempt to put you into boxes, into categories. We like to see these as mere placeholders rather than as terms that define us. We would feel trapped if we had to declare: this is who we are, this is what we are doing, and this is what we are about.

sw I appreciate your underscoring the relationship between judgment and values. Both are terms that have such negative, conservative connotations, but without determining preferences (judgments, biases) and the reasons for them (values), design became willy-nilly very quickly. And I also appreciate the distinction you draw between real judgment—moving things forward—and petty trivialities: the superficiality of a thumbs up or thumbs down rather than a considered judgment. Finally, I understand your desire not to limit yourselves with a singular label. But it's undeniable that your practice right now is becoming consistent. In other words, you are at a moment where judgment need not pose a trap but instead might serve as an opportunity to articulate the contours of that consistency. It's why I find the timing of this conversation to be ideal. It's terribly exciting to see a practice defining itself through its practice.

Of course, it is incredibly helpful to hear how you read and discuss the work of others. Your own values emerge from the thickets of the particular, considered, and (importantly) elaborated distinctions you articulate between practitioners, between projects, and between disciplines. You look at everything, and you always look very carefully. This same keen level of observation must then feed your own projects.

ML When we study and taxonomize other practices, we like to consider at which stage within the design process the crux or essence of architecture begins to emerge. In the United States, the scope of architectural services is typically divided by Schematic Design, Design Development, and Construction Documentation phases. We think that in a practice such as Peter Eisenman's architecture emerges in the Schematic Design phase. For Frank Gehry and Rem Koolhaas it is in the Design Development phase. For Herzog & de Meuron, the Construction Documentation phase. This is a gross generalization and reduction of these practices, of course, but it reflects where their values are situated. In design studios at schools, emphasis is typically placed upon Schematic Design. But we think it is useful to acknowledge that design does not have to solely reside within the conceptual phases of a project.

SW That's an interesting categorization and a provocative invitation to rethink these stages. So is Johnston Marklee consistent in terms of when a project gets articulated as a project: is it in Schematic Design or Construction Documentation? It seems you leave that a little bit open. Is that openness deliberate? Is there ever an office-wide discussion, or a discussion between the two of you, regarding the *project* underlying any given project? If so, when does that discussion take place?

To be clear, I fully understand that you do not adopt the same bias or judgment, or even the same perspective in every project. That lack of rigidity in your practice is liberating, but given the output of your office, we are also at a moment when you have enough work to begin to see certain commonalities emerging.

ML In some of our first works—the Hill House, the Sale House, the Walden Wilson Studio, or the group of projects in Marfa—the project came into being in the schematic stage. Firstly, because it was very clear in the beginning, given the limitations and circumstances of the commissions, that the challenges lay in the schematic design. Secondly, this group of projects took place during the infancy of our practice, when we felt a lack of security and that we had not yet mastered the process of construction. So we wanted to take our time in understanding the construction and what our situation would afford us to do.

Johnston Marklee, Walden Wilson Studio, Culver City, California, 2003.

sɪ   At the beginning of our practice we deliberately selected
and developed projects that allowed us to delve into and
refine our knowledge of building. The scope of research and
experimentation we were comfortable with has evolved over
time. While many younger architects tend to put every trick
they have ever dreamt of into their early projects, we wanted
to take our time and see what was possible in each situation.
In our case this included exploring issues such as the spatial
and architectural consequences of mass, profile, and edges;
the erasure of the frame; and material assemblies resulting in
a kind of muteness. We do not see the lack of articulation as
a reductive effort but more as a way to find the most direct
solution to a design problem. This research was, in part, a response to our local West Coast history, in which an abundance
of eclectic materials and iconic tectonic expression continue
to come into play. We were also aware that a lot of practices
around us were doing developed and complex surfaces, and
so we thought maybe we did not need to start there.

COLLECTING AND EDITING   sw   Your eschewing of the complex makes me think of how
                                  it was that Robert Venturi came to the topic of context in
                                  his Princeton MFA thesis in 1950: he realized then, looking
                                  around him, that no one was engaging the topic of context.
                                  Abstraction—or at least reduced articulation—was similarly
                                  absent from your scene, which made it especially interesting
                                  for you to take on.

ML   Have you seen Michael Blackwood's productions from the
nineteen-eighties, when he did a series of films on architects
like Peter Eisenman and Frank Gehry? He did one on Mies
van der Rohe, which came out in 1986, just when they recon-
structed the Barcelona Pavilion. The film was based on that
event but it was also documented Mies van der Rohe's entire
career. In the film they interviewed everybody from Dirk Lohan,
to Philip Johnson, to Peter Eisenman, and all of these men
spoke about Mies's influence on them. There was one scene
where they interviewed Robert Stern, who said that Mies did
not understand America, that America was not about austerity
but about dreams and fantasy, and that Mies obviously did
not know that. Right after Stern's interview it was Robert
Venturi's turn. You would expect Venturi to drop the bomb on
Mies but he said something like: "I reacted to Mies at the time
not because of Mies but all the followers of Mies. I think today
that all architects should worship at the feet of Mies van der
Rohe. I have said a lot of things in the past and I won't take
any of them back. The only thing that I will take back is that
'less is a bore.'"
     While one would usually group Stern and Venturi in the
same postmodern camp, their different positions toward Mies

created a schism within Postmodernism for me. These are the type of minute but decisive differences, similar to those between Thom Mayne and Frank Gehry, which mean a world to us.

sw I think that it is interesting trying to figure out how one in general and you two in particular differentiate positions and constantly recalibrate your own position within the constellation of contemporary practice. You are unusual among contemporary American practitioners because of your profound knowledge of architecture's history as well as its contemporary breadth. It's sad to say, but it's true—few practitioners of your generation take the time to read the field with the level of depth and nuance that you do. And they, in turn, don't profit as you do from that reading. Your ability to call out the difference between hardware manufacturers as well as the difference between Venturi's and Stern's particular reading of Mies—that knowledge base is typical of an older generation, perhaps partly because everyone feels that today you can call up information like this at a moment's notice, using Google, such that it's not necessary to take the time to parse nuance any more.

A level of connoisseurship is urgently needed to elevate critique beyond the simple thumbs up/thumbs down. At the same time, mere connoisseurship can be misunderstood as simplistic cataloging. And while this false connoisseurship often stands in for critique, extremely detailed knowledge is not the same thing as considered knowledge. Parsing into categories still requires the hard work of determining the *value*, to use your word, of those categories. That's where connoisseurship lies.

I would love to see you carve a path—a little red line— through all of your incredible knowledge of architecture, of art, of history, of the contemporary world, to render more visible where and how that knowledge has affected different projects. It would be like a web page with all the hyperlinks enabled: clicking on one project would reveal its intersections and resonances with so many other projects, things, histories, stories, et cetera. These connections are revealed in conversation with you; it would be great for others to get to enter that conversation.

sj We see our work as part of a continuum. The engagement with the discipline that you suggest gives us tremendous flexibility while, at the same time, it delineates disciplinary boundaries that can be traced historically. We thrive on these apparently oppositional parameters and use them as a base for invention. Approaching each project with a relatively broad disciplinary perspective inspires us to situate even our smallest projects into much larger or projective contexts to test the model at an urban or suburban scale. Or in the case of the View House, our strategy for apertures and mass was examined as a script to rewrite traditional suburban plot development profiles. We insert our work back into other contexts to potentially reconfigure the landscape around it materially, conceptually, or historically.

ML Decisions are made by measuring work against disciplinary models. Knowledge is a prelude to the formation of judgment.

SW Exactly. The more you know, the more you can make productive judgments. Strangely, though, some people feel the more they know the more paralyzing it can be. You two are unusually comfortable with making judgments. Trying to figure out how to render those judgments public is useful.

ML We do feel comfortable making judgments, as well as being reticent about the outcome. This relates to the issues of taste and connoisseurship, and the danger in being too self-conscious of one's taste. The collection of knowledge can be a precarious way to travel. You can be burdened by the knowledge to the point you cannot move forward anymore.

SW It can become a burden in a couple of senses. For example, it's easy to freeze up because all existing models appear to be so good that it's very hard to go beyond or to locate your own originality. The other way it can be a burden is by focusing too much on the perfection of the object as opposed to the object's role: like trapping butterflies just to have them in your collection, as opposed to understanding how they fly. I think that's where people can make assumptions about connoisseurship being too reductive a knowledge model. I do think that a map of your influences and resonances would form an extraordinary constellation of connoisseurship within and beyond architecture, which would constitute your line of judgment. Another revealing exercise would be to do an exhibition of your office's work that doesn't show each project sequentially but instead focuses on what happens when the projects start to live together, as they do in your office. Like little chunky beasts from some animated movie—I can't help but imagine that all the models in your office have all sorts of parties when the people have gone home.

ML Like the way James Stirling put all his projects within Nolli's Roman context in *Roma Interrotta*, which also reminds me of OMA's aerial drawing of Berlin with their Checkpoint Charlie project drawn within a fictitious context of the city. It included built works such as Schinkel's Schauspielhaus along with unbuilt works such as Mies van der Rohe's tower, Ludwig Hilberseimer's slabs on Friedrichstrasse, and the completed Metalworkers Union Building by Erich Mendelsohn.

James Stirling, *Roma Interrotta* exhibition, Rome, Italy, final drawing, between 1977 and 1979, ink on reprographic copy (88.5×139cm).

sw   In an ideal world, what would you want to ideally be adjacent to your project? Right now, the way you present implies that the only ideal neighbor is nature. I don't think that's true. If I saw the drawings and slides of your project without hearing you, I would think that the designer were from the Pacific Northwest or Northern California and really believed in nature, and I don't think of you as nature folk so much— you're both more city folk. Even those collages of the dotted lines and the views, would you want to see the Sears Tower or the Hancock Tower in those images? There is room for fiction that enables you to suggest a possible city, even if you don't have the commission to design a city.

ML   We are interested in collecting, whether neighbors, fellow travelers, or knowledge. We start collecting fragments of knowledge without particular purposes and collect until the disparate pieces of information come together to form a pattern. This gives us a historical perspective and creates a certain critical distance. We are generally interested in things that are slightly less popular, less mainstream in architecture. We are very aware of what is emerging in architecture, but it helps to have a little buffer from it in order to take the time to digest and understand. We think being one step ahead or one step behind is more interesting than being right here and now all the time.

SJ   We find that distancing ourselves from the work in the design process, through the lens of other practices, opens up new ways to develop and connect material and research paths. Collecting is essential to this kind of process because it is not a linear practice and often involves accidents and surprises. Holding on to information, objects, and ideas, intuitively grasping their importance, sometimes before recognizing their value, is fundamental to our work.

sw   It strikes me that you two can offer an approach to how you think others (students, but also colleagues working in architecture and design internationally) might deal with today's information overload. How might you promote a particularly twenty-first-century mode of connoisseurship appropriate to today's fast economy of information? When you and Sharon were on the roof of the Standard Hotel for the Postopolis event you made an interesting point about the difference between media and architecture and their differing paces: you said that architecture, in particular, needs to know which issues it can best address and which ones are better addressed by other media. In other words, architecture should not try to do everything; it's best suited to do certain things. It's a smart point, and you articulated it very effectively.

SJ   Mark's description of how we collect and assimilate information as a generative practice already suggests our propensity for considering information in groups and clusters—in orbits, even. Inherent to collecting are notions of originals and replicas, multiples, and families or colonies— taxonomies of material. The curatorial dimension of how we collect and edit information also suggests that what we edit out is as important as what is included.

sw   I find it fascinating to try to imagine an urban version of your project. Do your projects need an antithesis to define a difference or would they work better for you as a series of forms? What happens not only when you increase the scale of your work, but also when you multiply it? So much of your work consists of singular objects. Do you ever take on projects at an urban scale?

ML   I think in a large urban scale our projects might be like proverbial needles in the haystack. Nevertheless, I feel our projects, particularly recently, address the scale of the city. In the scale of our singular buildings, the chunkiness, stubbiness, or "stumpy-ness" aspires to an awkwardness and incompletion that inevitably promote their own multiplication. We have looked at the tension between the object and the city through the masques of John Hejduk. In his *Berlin Masque* series there were existing buildings that he placed his projects around, and then in *Victims*, a second version, where there is absolutely nothing. All the buildings are hinged together, huddling together to form tension between the objects. There is something incredible in the way these buildings straddle the role of participant and observer of the city.

John Hejduk, *Berlin Masque*, site plan, 1981, ink on translucent paper (118.3 × 107.5 cm).

John Hejduk, *Victims*, composite site plan, 1984, pen and black ink on paper (ca. 137 × 197 cm).

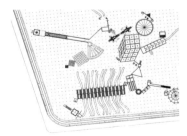

John Hejduk, *Victims*, 1984, detail.

sw   To what extent does your project, which could be characterized as an autonomous object-oriented project, get hurt by multiplication? Or by a change in scale?

ML This model that transcends scales reminds us of Aldo Rossi in that the arrangement of a cigarette box, a coffee pot, and a can of soda could be seen as a proto-urban model. Rafael Moneo once commented that Rossi's architecture of the city is the backdrop for life to happen. By contrast, in Hejduk's view of the city buildings are not just in the background but rather become part of life without imposing on life itself. And subsequently, the fragility in the bases of Hejduk's buildings suggests that they are always on the move, transient and never really grounded. His series of masque projects stems from this desire for buildings to be nomadic, mobile objects.

Aldo Rossi, *Untitled*, 1981.

SW It is interesting that you admire the nomadic quality in Hedjuk's work, given the implication of heaviness that your projects convey. Even the Hill House, which looks like it's being puffed up with air and is about to float away, is very anchored to its site. We talked about levitation, that something might be at once very anchored and appear as if it could move.

ML We believe that weight, whether physical weight or visual weight, is always dynamic. Equilibrium could be considered to be a state of stasis, but we are interested in achieving a dynamic equilibrium instead of a static equilibrium. In the Hill House we wanted the building to appear grounded but just at the threshold of tipping over. It is about treating gravity as both an asset and a liability.

This text is based on conversations held in Houston on February 10, 2012 and in Los Angeles on February 16, 2012.

Hill House

DESIGN YEARS
2002

CONSTRUCTION YEARS
2003–2004

LOCATION
Pacific Palisades, California, United States

SITE AREA
460 m² / 4,950 sf

FLOOR AREA
334 m² / 3,600 sf

CLIENT
Chan Luu

PRINCIPALS
Sharon Johnston and Mark Lee

PROJECT TEAM
Jeff Adams, Mark Rea Baker, Diego
Arraigada, Brennan Buck, Michelle Cintron,
Daveed Kapoor, Anne Rosenberg, Anton
Schneider, Ruth Hügli

STRUCTURAL ENGINEER
William Koh and Associates

CONTRACTOR
Hinerfeld-Ward, Inc.

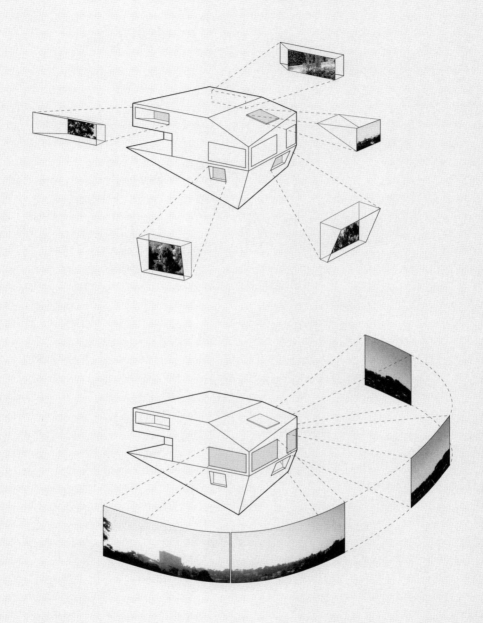

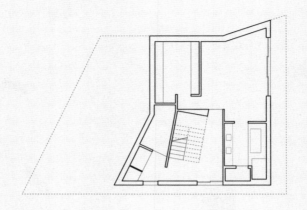

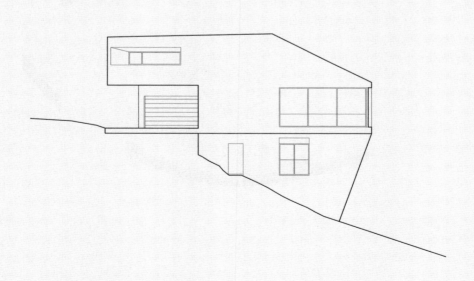

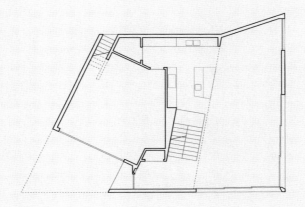

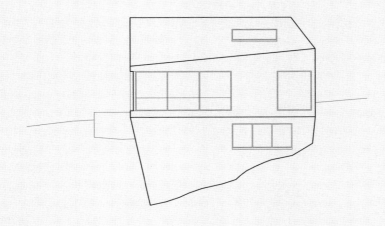

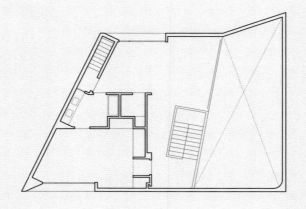

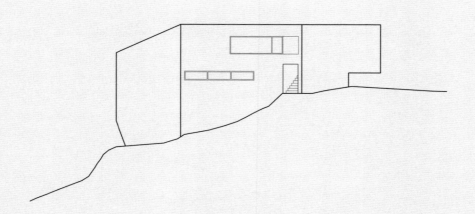

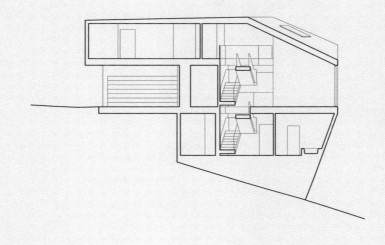

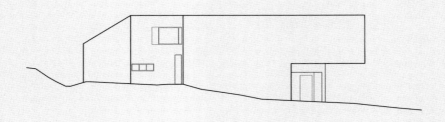

Insert

Walead Beshty

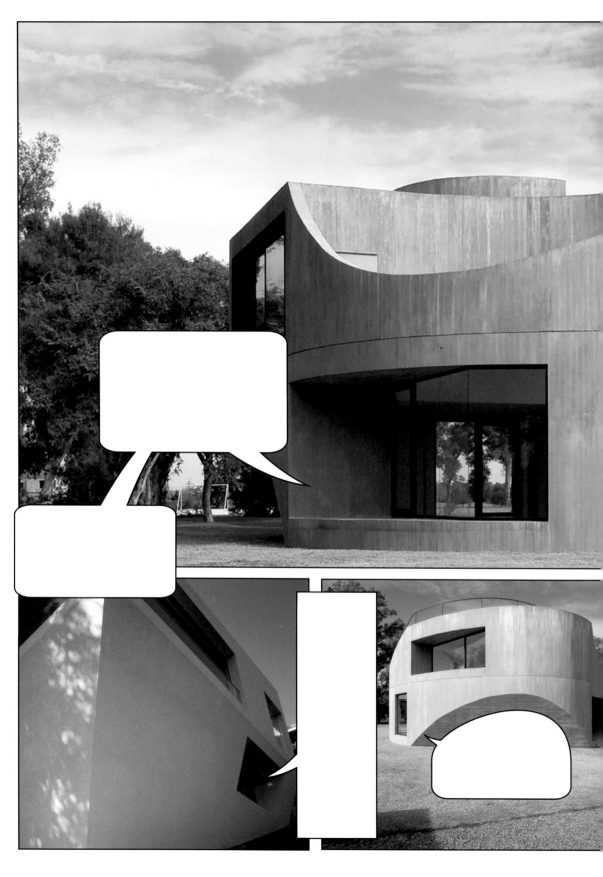

IV)

On Multiplicity

Sharon Johnston and Mark Lee in conversation with

BLESS
Desiree Heiss
Ines Kaag

ML   We have followed your work since the beginning; we started around the same time as you did and we are a duo, as you are. I think we see BLESS as a parallel practice to our own and we look at your work to be inspired and surprised. While we primarily design buildings and you design clothing, accessories, and furniture, there is a way in which you approach your work that we find fascinating. Johnston Marklee and BLESS—two practices, two pairs. Let's begin by talking about our concepts of collaboration, by discussing the specific way you approach your work, both the collaboration between the two of you and in the collaborations you form with others.

DH   BLESS collaborations with other partners generally happen in two ways. Either companies like Wrangler or Oxbow, for example, approach us, or—though not usually—we think about whom we could team up with next. We consider collaborations in terms of what they can provide, possibly a product we are normally are not able to produce in that kind of a price range, like in the case of the Wrangler pants.

IK   For BLESS №12, for example, the "Team-up" type, we wanted to collaborate with a set of different companies, to join forces and coproduce a variety of projects. In the end we also think egoistically about obsessive technical issues: referring to the collaboration with Wrangler, we wanted to find out how to improve the cut, or how to make jeans look like jeans. In the end it is about the finishing. It is all about details, things like the length of the stitching that separates designer jeans from sportswear jeans.

BLESS №34 Wrangler Looks, Adrien
Wrangler's classic combined with elements
of BLESS.

BLESS №12 Team-ups
Materialmix Jewelry.

SJ   Our interest in your collaboration also lies in the way the two of you work together and how you communicate across distance. There is often not only distance between you two physically but also a kind of distance between two concepts or materials, as in the Wrangler jeans project, for example. Finding something fruitful in the differences between things by using very specific tools to combine them and turn them into something more special is very familiar. For us, part of the collaborative project is to create an open-minded and open-ended atmosphere, something without a predetermined result that allows for moments of surprise.

DH   Architects have to work with so many teams to get their projects built; how does Johnston Marklee engage collaboration both within and outside of your office? How do you approach collaboration differently given that architects often necessarily team up with engineers, landscape architects, and other experts?

ML   Within the office we try to start each project in a fresh way. We build up a sensibility about the project from a wide range of sources, while also tapping into the orbits of ideas circling around the office. We seek out collaborations to see things in different ways. We like talking about architectural problems with those who have very different formal and visual languages than we do. For example, artists Walead Beshty and Juliao Sarmento, or scientists like Jim Gymzewski, or the Housing Secretary Shaun Donovan, to name just a few. We find such conversations challenging, unforgiving, and inspiring.

Johnston Marklee with Walead Beshty, *Later Layer*, Italian Cultural Institute, Los Angeles, 2010.

IK   Collaborations in fashion are frequently enforced by marketing departments that ask designers to come up with a product or project for something new. In our work with Charles Jourdan and New Balance this was a particular challenge— without support from the marketing department it is hard to move forward with these companies.

BLESS Nº06 Costumizable Footwear Limited Edition with New Balance & Charles Jourdain.

ML This seems to suggest that collaboration could become part of one's identity or public persona.

IK When we worked with H&M and Adidas we asked them to donate stuff. Although we called these collaborations, for them the projects were actually more like donations. They passed on the garments and we reworked them.

BLESS №10 Scarf-double. Rawmanagement, H&M.

ML These different modes of collaboration you have referred to—relay races, as with H&M and Adidas, or reciprocal processes like the projects with Wrangler and Oxbow—could migrate from fashion to architecture. It is about channeling each collaborator's expertise or naïveté toward the product.

SJ At the core of each architectural project are very real—one could even say mundane—concerns and requirements. Casting a wide net of research and collaborative discourse creates the complexity of ingredients to distill a rich and unexpected context for each project.

ML There are two aspects of your work we would like to discuss: the classic and the ready-made, two concepts in which we also have great interest. How do you relate your design approach to those concepts?

READY-MADES AND CLASSICS

IK We would not call it ready-made design but, rather, some sort of ready-made style. We are interested in common sense. We have an agreement that if something seems good to us there is no need to redesign it just for the sake of changing a minor detail. Sometimes these adjustments have to be made, for example when we work on pants and we need to define if the pleat is here or there. But, ultimately, we do not care so much about those concerns and simply try to make the product look good. If we could work with the most classic production places we would, of course, do that. But for organizational reasons it is impossible for us to go to the most sophisticated Italian house where they tailor the best jackets. We could simply not afford it. Style-wise there is a certain range of products—even beyond clothes—we don't see the need to redesign. For a chair, for example, we would not draw its legs in a 3D CAD program. It is much easier and nicer, and

220

better fits our concept, to simply find a classic chair, take its legs off, and use them for our own chair.

ML We totally agree that certain things are just right the way they are. The focus of the project is then on the framing of that element in a new context with a new purpose, which initiates a transformation process.

SJ This focus in architecture is often about innovation. For us, a discussion of innovation usually starts with notions of the classic. Issues of the classic relate to our preoccupation with history and the disciplinary boundaries that form the framework for our thinking. There are certain parameters which are unwavering for us, bounds that exist at the core of the discipline. At the same time, we find new ways to look at these issues of type, for example by colonizing seemingly forgotten peripheral positions or parallel practices. Instead of beginning a design project with a top-down typological approach or a vague heuristic model, we begin to approximate a type through design development and move toward the model through approximation.

IK BLESS style is not about real ready-mades, but more about classics in the sense that we do not want to redesign classics. For the "Prince Charles Blazer," we wanted to work with the best manufacturing house in order to get the most classic look possible. It should be perceived as a high-class product of good quality, but not one that makes you think about the length of the stitches.

BLESS Nº47 Prince Charles jacket, brown, reflector.

BLESS Nº47 Prince Charles jacket, night.

ML I've heard you mention that while you are not against cashmere sweaters, per se, you also don't feel the need in the market to produce another beautiful cashmere sweater.

BLESS seems both to operate with a specific level of high-end production and to question the typical framework within which this production typically happens in the conservative market.

IK The thing about the cashmere sweater is that we will simply do a small, self-serving re-edition. After we produced some V-necks and round necks in the very beginning, we received many requests over the years to produce more extended collections. Also, the ones we were wearing for six years are quite worn out by now. Of course, we stick to our key concept and want only to create things not available on the market but, in this case, we by chance found the perfect yarn and shape which needed to prove its *raison d'être* over years until we were more convinced than ever that a luxury product such as this one satisfies basic needs of grounded contemporaries (*Zeitgenossen*). And because there is no time for extended research on where to obtain a similar quality product, we decided to produce it again, but this time consciously considering the fact that only a small fan base is willing to buy one good sweater instead of five affordable ones.

DH How do issues of your "industry," and the facts of standardized products, dimensions, and processes inform your work?

SJ From early in our career there were certain things we wanted to focus on that others seemed not to be considering. At the same time there are many limitations: budgets and schedules and things that were external givens for each project. After working in Europe for several years, we realized that window profiles were one of the first clues as to whether a building was American or European. The European frames are typically much thinner and more elegant (the parallel would be stitching in fashion). Without budgets for such elegant window constructions or the interest to customize them as industrial design objects, our focus shifted away from the window specification—it became like a ready-made—to the overall mass of the building.

ML The issues of the classic and the ready-made within the design process have preoccupied us for a long time. I was an English boarding school student and wore uniforms and ties. So my general sartorial sensibility is based on very classic values. I first understood BLESS through the classical pieces like "Prince Charles," a piece which many might not consider typical in relation to your more progressive designs. But the jacket became my entry into the BLESS world and it later allowed me to understand the more daring pieces, like the big pleated pants. Sharon, on the other hand, grew up in Malibu and has a *sportive* disposition, so the sportier pieces became her entry. We appreciate the fact of these two entry points and we aspire to a similar quality in our work. While critics

BLESS Nº36, Mark Lee wearing BLESS.

222

tend to put us in one camp or another, our work is situated in a more expanded history of ideas and forms.

BLESS Nº51 Look, Gloria.

DH We completely understand this. There was a group of people who were totally confused when "Prince Charles" appeared. They wondered what it was and envisioned our label to do fashion like Comme de Garçons. And it worked similarly with the sports aspect. For us it was somehow groundbreaking because this kind of female sportswear based mainly on a traditional male wardrobe was rare to find. We do not want to create sportswear in the classic sense. We thought about the idea of being both female and quite sporty at the same time, which makes the design of evening gowns obsolete, because we do not go out and we would not need them ourselves. We wanted to have clothing in which we were comfortable, clothing produced at a level of quality that we could accept. We were aiming for garments in which you feel good but in which you do not necessarily attract a lot of attention. In a sense, we tend to design things we would want to wear ourselves. Does this sound familiar to you? How do your lives, your practice, and your work interact?

BLESS Nº51 Look, Beate.

SJ Your work is probably more autobiographical than ours is. For us, as architects, almost every project is a commission. We never start from a clean slate. We have to deal with many external contingencies but we continuously build up a loose and wide-ranging collection of research ideas that exist beyond the specific parameters of a project. I recall a meeting with a large committee that was selecting the architect for a new building. One member of the group asked us very earnestly what we would do if we were selected and, in the design process, they asked us to change the position of a window. Because they felt our approach was so personal they feared that they would essentially have no place in the process. Our work is highly specific but it is built up from a supple and expansive context of information and research that provides us with the necessary flexibility in the design process. We are convinced that strong work needs a clear framework, often defined through the plan, to eventually embody a generous quality capable of absorbing factors we will never be able to control once a project is complete and occupied. This range of liberating and controlling aspects is part of the exciting discovery and surprise of all things BLESS does. We learn new ways to wear pieces, with buttoning, draping, and tying, very basic facts of garment architecture, but each piece becomes so personal for each individual and is almost unrecognizable from person to person. On one level the work is very obsessive and specific and, on another, it is quite free and malleable. We find those qualities to represent another definition of luxury.

ART AND THE UN-VISUAL

DH   The open-ended quality of our work often requires us to explain it a million times verbally; the fashion industry is not used to "un-visual" fashion. For many people in the industry, fashion is either classic or up to date with trends or it possesses a strong visual statement. But then there are those who are aware of fashion and not necessarily interested in it just to make a statement or to show that they know what is going on. This group is hard to define. They posses a certain awareness for clothes, they care about what they wear, and while what they wear is important to them it does not serve as an important tool of communication. They do not reach out to claim: "Look at my clothes and you know what I am thinking." You must also have this community who understands your work.

SJ   This term "un-visual" is very relevant because creative products, from architecture to fashion, are consumed at a very fast pace by means of images. We find that critics, clients, and writers often take a long time to understand our work because it cannot be easily labeled. The Vault House, for example, is always described as bold but not visible on the surface. We embrace the slowness of architecture in the design, building, and experiencing of it. We consider the delayed judgment that comes with such slowness an opportunity to discover and build depth into the experience of our work.

Johnston Marklee, Vault House, Oxnard, California, 2013.

224

Johnston Marklee, Vault House, Oxnard, California, 2013.

DH   This actually describes a good costume. You should not pay attention to a costume in a movie. It should not speak by itself but should absolutely support its purpose.

ML   Kristin Burke, who served as costume designer of the movie *The Cooler* (2003), described how she designed seven suits for William H. Macy, the protagonist who starts off really down and out and then, at the end, wins everything. She created the same suit in seven different cuts. In the beginning the suit was very ill fitting, so the character looked a little bit out of place. But then, toward the end of the movie, the suit was perfectly tailored. Burke explained that it was due to the different degrees of fit that one was not able to notice how the tailoring work evolved with the development of the character in the story. After we heard her explain her technique we watched the movie again and you can clearly see the development from the beginning to the end, when the protagonist somehow looks bespoke and exquisite.

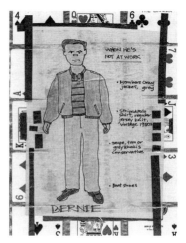

Kristin M. Burke, costume design for the movie *The Cooler*, "When he's not at work."

Kristin M. Burke, costume design for the movie *The Cooler*, "When he's cool."

225

SJ   Martha Graham insists that the dancers in her avant-garde dance company be classically trained. She feels it is crucial to be trained in classic ballet to have a good sense of center. Or, in the mid-eighties, when Jean Paul Gaultier first started, men's skirts were the big thing. He designed them with the most traditional materials and patterns, like window plaids. I thought this contrast was interesting. And it is something similar that we find in the work of BLESS, this contrast and coexistence of the rear-guard and the avant-garde.

Jean Paul Gaultier wearing one of his skirts at the Cali Exposhow, Colombia, 2012.

DH   I would even go further and describe it is as a profound need to work with classic elements. This is quite easy for us because it is as if they were a predefined value that we can relate to. And we do not have to think about it design-wise. It is there, we like it, and we use it.

ML   It is not a matter of creating it. It is much rather a matter of what you can add to a larger, ongoing project. Most people say that in order to create the next new thing they have to personify it. I remember that a long time ago Sharon was looking at a *BLESS Look Book* and noticed that BLESS has no desire to be sexy. This observation intrigued me; maybe it's another aspect of un-visual fashion.

DH   It's funny that you say that. Just the other day I read an old issue of a French magazine that was entirely dedicated to Tom Ford. It was a very nice issue and, surprisingly, I liked it. It was so interesting because Ford was very emotional throughout his career and also had a very close relationship with his partner. He explained how he had been dying to know what his partner thought about his first show at Gucci, and that his partner replied that just a little bit of sexiness added to the whole thing would help him to succeed. Tom Ford claims this was a key moment. It made him understand that he could not go anywhere without "sexiness." That is why you make me laugh when you mention it.

ML   BLESS has absolutely no desire to be sexy? A degree-zero sexiness?

DH   Sexiness is important in fashion, but in the art world it is even an obsession. It's just everywhere there. It is so important, this "sex" thing.

SJ   But BLESS has been well received in the art world, which reminds me of a funny story. During Art Basel Miami a few years ago a chic gallery director chased me through the fair asking: "What are you wearing, what are you wearing?" I had BLESS on and she had to completely undress me to look at every piece I was wearing. I think the fact that my style was unlike anyone else's fascinated her (un-visually). She found vaguely familiar details and pieces but it was not a *Vogue* look; it was not a formula. How each person wears and layers the clothes with his or her own style and body is essential to how the pieces come to life. This is the BLESS magic and a quality that inspires us, as designers. As a corollary we know there is only a certain level of control we can have as architects. Much of the experience is left to those who occupy the spaces we design. The strong form and structure of the Hill House, for example, registers a specific volume of space relative to this particular site in the canyon. But the interior spaces are very casual and can absorb and transform very different kinds of styles of living and types of activities. The house feels animated and engaging when you are there alone or when it is full of people. It is a generous space. More people in the art world responded to this than people in the architectural world.

Johnston Marklee, Hill House, Los Angeles, 2004, photograph by Julius Shulman.

IK   Yes, that's true. More people in the art world might be aware of our work than in the fashion world.

ML   So, in a way, you occupy an alternative position. Is this niche market something that you want to maintain?

IK   No. For us it is actually not so important.

ML   The reception of it is not so important? Do you feel that it would affect and change your thinking if you were too self-conscious about it?

IK   Ideally it works in the sense that it generates an economic basis but there is no direct commercial purpose. We never sat down and said: "OK, let's do it this way, let's add a little bit of style and combine it with furniture and architecture." This is not what we are good at. We collaborate, and we talk a lot about what would be nice to do one day, but our time is very limited. We strongly believe in our ideas and have the will to see what comes of them. Take BLESS Nº26 Cable Jewelry, for example: we took everyday computer cables, extension cords, and transformers and turned these things into jewelry through beading or weaving or crocheting. We became extremely excited to work with these everyday objects. Everybody needs a power strip and thinks about how to hide it or how to make it look nice. We felt that we succeeded with a strong idea that offered many different variations. It didn't work in the beginning. And it took a long time before people started to realize that it was good that finally someone tackled it. But, initially, people did not buy it. It took a long time to make them understand that we would also provide a service furnishing the cables directly in an office space.

BLESS Nº26 Cable Jewelry.

DH   It is a nice project in the sense that you see the strength of an idea when it is copied. About two years ago there was a bigger company that started to produce decorated cables in a very basic way. It is quite nice because it is not a really major design scope. It is such a small intervention.

ML   The Cable Jewelry is an interesting example of the fact that your concepts are very democratic. People can see it and say: "I can understand it, or I thought about it, but BLESS made it happen."

DH   Indeed, there are so many interns who work with us who do millions of Cable Jewelry pieces when they have spare time and they start to do their own variations.

ML   Who would you say are your influences or inspirations?   REFERENCE
Whether from the past or the present, artists and designers, or other creative fields like literature?

DH   We do not have direct references for our work. They are cultural or temporal. There are a lot of people we respect or we would like to do work for. For example, we both like the dancer Pina Bausch but it's not like one of her performances inspired a particular piece.

ML   So, influences are absorbed, digested, and filtered through your lives before informing the work.

DH   It is more like a momentary experience that could happen now. When I arrived at the BLESS office there was a recent *Look Book* left open in front of the toilet on the bathroom floor and I don't think anyone left it open.

IK   No; that was actually me. I was reading it in the bathroom and left it there on the floor.

BLESS Lookbook edition.

DH   Oh, I thought that the book might have fallen down accidentally and opened up like this. In any case, I immediately started thinking about stone books on the stone floor, a type of floor decoration that is immediately open and present when you sit down. It is in this kind of situation, when you are not thinking of anything, that you discover a specific constellation of things and you think that it just fits on this particular spot on the ground.

ML   I saw the book in the bathroom too but I did not want to touch it because it was right in front of the toilet and open to a certain page.

DH   This is funny; you go to a toilet and you don't think of anything specific and then suddenly you think precisely about this book. At first I thought reading a poem would be nice, but then you would have to turn the pages. That is why I was thinking of a stone variation. It is this little moment that makes you contemplate.

IK   Do you manage to see exhibitions, to read books, to listen to music? I feel that there is no time to see anything. I am happy if I can turn on the radio in the morning and listen to it. Would you see an exhibition and then think of the next concept for a house? Do you feel inspired by exhibitions you see or by other artists, for example? We get asked this question so often that we feel a bit arrogant to always say no. Nothing inspires me. We do not care. I think Desiree gave a good example with the book in the bathroom. It could be that you are standing in a dense crowd and you see a seam and then you think about how it would look from two meters away.

DH Inspiration from established artists or architects is related to our previous discussion of classic products. You see something, you admire it, you even adore it, and you think it is fantastic, but it's already done! We don't want to include it in our work. We just like it as it is.

ML When people talk to us they want to understand us in a context, whether it is the artistic or intellectual community. With whom and to what are we connected? Where does the work come from? Who are our forefathers?

IK Can you give us an example of things that inspired you and how they can be directly connected to your work?

ML Most of our projects originated in commissions. We inherit a situation, a site, and a problem. When we are working on a project we may go to an art show or read about a project. The artist may have dealt with a quality of space or material or a concept in a way that is parallel with a situation we have and may help us think about our situation in a different way.

SJ We are always collecting and organizing reference material, which we understand as part of our practice. This work never translates directly to a design solution, but the material builds a kind of aura around a project and our collective design thinking as a team. In architecture there are so many technical, top-down problems to solve. For us it is about unlearning. It is about letting go of things to liberate our thinking. It is about forgetting how to do it the industry way, to allow for something else to come into play, something that informs a transformation.

DH To unlearn is a nice term—the implication is that you have to know something in order to forget it.

ML The collaborative teaching workshops we did in Berlin were an interesting experience for me, and an opportunity to unlearn. If I had taught the students by myself the results would have become very object-oriented at the end. Seeing and understanding the process was important. While we recognize process as an important dimension in our work, it is very easy to prematurely focus on what we have to deliver. Sometimes we intentionally seek opportunities to collaborate, or situations that contaminate our routine, or things that are outside of what we normally do. In order to unlearn.

BLESS, Mark Lee at the collaborative teaching workshop Berlin.

IK But it is true that it makes a big difference—in architecture even more than in furniture design—that there are things like structures you have to solve. There is a big responsibility on a technical level.

SJ Yes, our challenge is to absorb all the technical matters in such a way that they disappear into the experience of the space. We want to be like magicians; we want you to forget where the structure is working hard. We want you to be surprised by the illusions.

This text is based on a conversation held in Berlin on May 7, 2011.

Porch House

DESIGN YEARS
2011–2012

CONSTRUCTION YEARS
2012–2013

LOCATION
Los Angeles, California, United States

SITE AREA
2,448 m² / 26,350 sf

FLOOR AREA
590 m² / 6,360 sf

CLIENT
Laurie David

PRINCIPALS
Sharon Johnston and Mark Lee

PROJECT TEAM
Anton Schneider, Katrin Terstegen, Lindsay
Erickson, Gary Ku, Ian Thomas, Mie Benson,
Philipp Breuer

STRUCTURAL ENGINEER
Simpson Gumpertz & Heger Inc.

CONTRACTOR
RJC Builders, Inc.

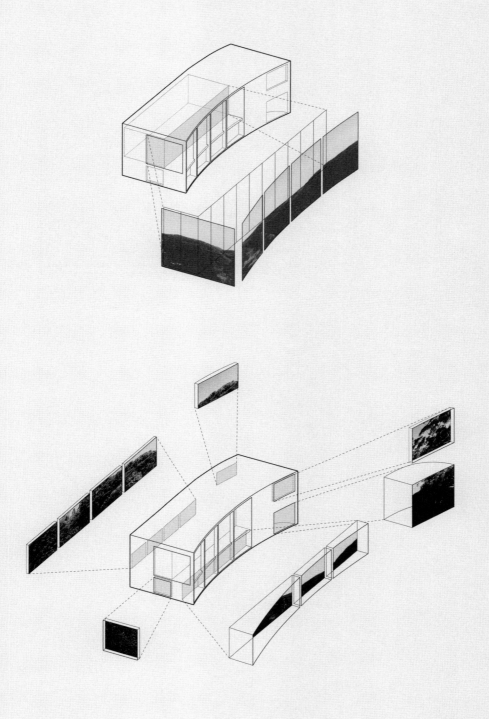

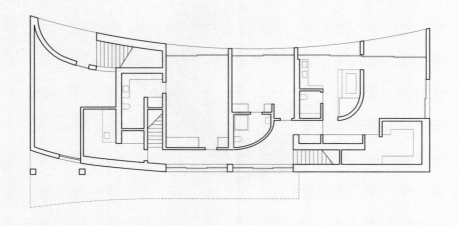

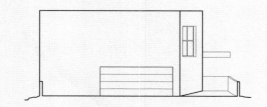

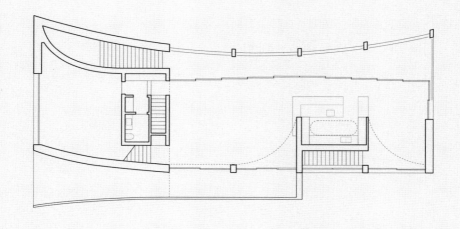

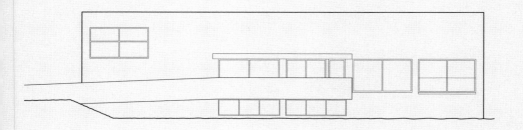

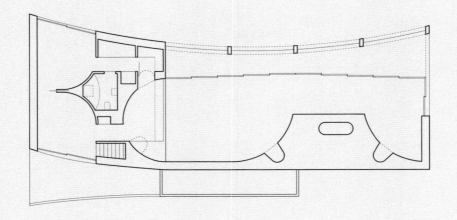

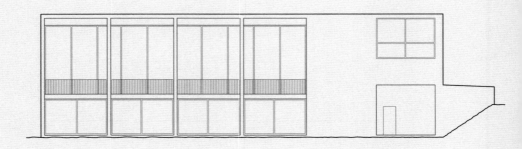

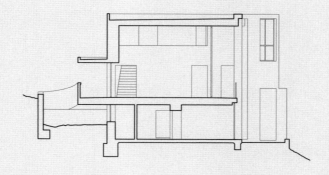

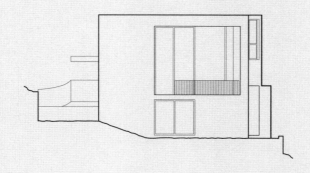

Vault House
Oxnard
California
2013

Portrait

Jack Pierson

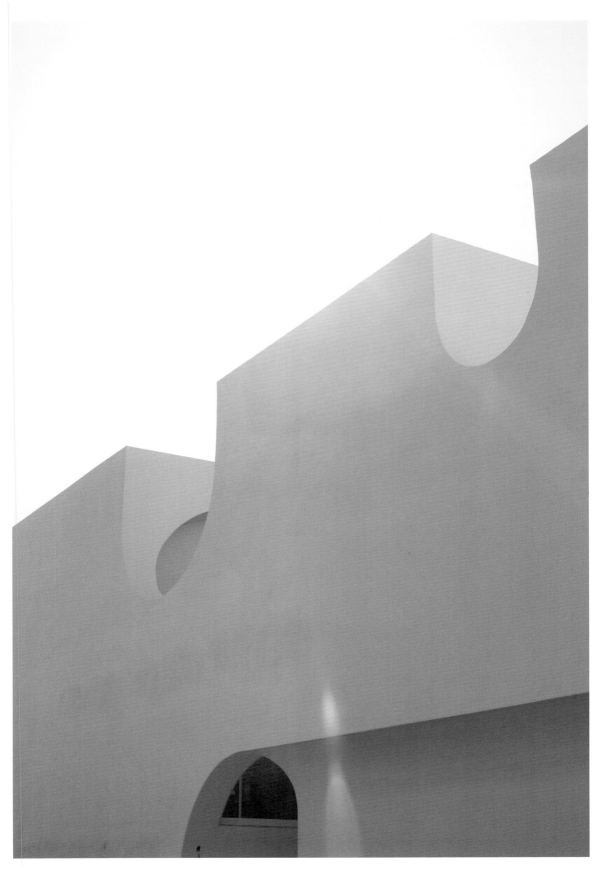

V)

On Geometry

Sharon Johnston and Mark Lee in conversation with

Sylvia Lavin

SL One of the most consistent aspects of how you present—and produce—your work is that it seems nothing is ever alone. You describe individual works as belonging to a family of possible objects, you proceed in relation to typologies that precede you, and you frame your ideas in relation to the ideas of others. Nothing is alone. Even when the situation depends on an isolated site or a problem that appears to be *sui generis*, you work hard to bring somebody or something else in to ensure that there is no "aloneness." Every step of the process seems to move by way of a collaboration or by phenomena that are doubled if not trebled. Of course, you also belong to a generation in which the single architect has given way to more collective producing agents. When I speak of you, "you" are already doubled in a way that reflects importantly on the state of contemporary cultural production.

ML I remember the piece you wrote in *Arquitectura Viva* about how Frank Gehry is an outsider—someone who is outside and inside at the same time. We are always part of an architectural community but we also always feel a little outside. Maybe this is a position that we are quite comfortable with and one that also differs in the American community versus in the European community. European colleagues tend to think that we are very American and American colleagues perceive us to be very European. As a consequence, we never really felt we belonged or were attached to a particular group or movement. So, we began to reach out to other fields early on. The art world became a way for us not to limit ourselves to a single community, but rather to take part in a much less political and more direct exchange about the work and how it communicates. It started off innocently with projects in Marfa, working with art institutions and collectors; it led to collaborations with artists and evolved from there. Artists from the nineteen-sixties and seventies were so engaged with notions of specificity and with the concreteness of things in the world. We find that directness relevant to our thinking.

Johnston Marklee, Amiryani Residence, Marfa, Texas, 2003.

SL It is interesting that the person who first comes to mind is Gehry. Certainly Gehry worked hard to become an auteur against a context that rewarded corporate bureaucracy and its valorization of economic efficiency. For him, a strong and individualized voice was necessary to resist forces of anonymization. On the other hand, this outsider status produced a form of camaraderie—his famous group of artist friends who also considered themselves outsiders—that was useful to him as an architect. Outside the world of bureaucratic architecture he found or, better yet, constructed for himself a confraternity of outsiders, a band of brethren, who in turn led him to a new inside. Clement Greenberg and others wrote this dynamic of the outsider/insider into the history of the

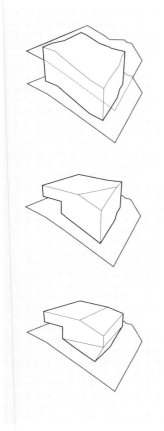

Johnston Marklee, Hill House, Los Angeles, 2004, massing.

avant-garde. Greenberg describes how early-twentieth-century artists isolated themselves from contemporary society by moving to Bohemia, but found new forms of collectivity in this alleged social isolation.

Your work raises similar dilemmas but in a new cadence. You often use words like "familiar"—not a term associated with the historical avant-gardes or even with what some have described as Robert Venturi and Denise Scott Brown's neo-avant-gardist interest in vernacular contextualism (they saw the vernacular as a way to produce new specialness rather than familiarity). On the other hand, through your deliberate effort to be visually low to the ground, to blend in, you communicate resistance to what you frame as the dominant tendency for architecture to seek iconicity. In this move away from the singular status of the object, you find new ways to insist that you are not alone.

This sort of operation seems especially pertinent to the Hill House. Although Hill House is not a collaboration, not a collective project in traditional terms, the house occupies not only Pierre Koenig's design but actually lives in Julius Schulman's photograph of this other house: you appropriate both as posthumous collaborators. The way you talk about zoning has similar effects. You present zoning as though it naturally forced you to do this or that but in so invoking the code at every turn, you transform zoning into a kind of alter ego that becomes a partner in the process. This critique of the single and often heroic figure of the architect places you deeply within your architectural generation. Of course the irony is that this kind of critique, or rather the figure of non-heroic architect, is now engendering its own forms of notoriety.

sj   The Hill House was our first publicized project and, in our early practice, we became identified with it, including the rhetoric about the zoning code and the representational connection to Schulman. In the View House, the issue of geometry implicated construction and methods of making form. We were exploring how to make a building language of form and material that can engage a rural context without being mimetic or familiar. It strives to engage but remains unfamiliar. In this sense, the building doesn't blend in but rather fits in loosely, while maintaining a formal autonomy. It is the balance of these contrasting conditions that we find interesting to pursue. In many ways it is not unlike our collaborations with artists; there is a loose fit that allows each to maintain autonomy. It allows us to remain outsiders, between disciplines and locales. In a way we isolate ourselves further through collaborations; we find this is productive.

ml   One way or another, we change or transform the context in which we work. For instance, the generation before us had a very defined style. That previous generation positioned themselves as demiurgic, heroic, avant-garde figures. So, at the outset, we tried to avoid any overriding style. We certainly benefit from their work and research, but we also see a lot of them burn. So how do you take this vision and cloak it in a different way, as a critique of the iconic singular author? At our lectures, people frequently ask why we aren't doing complex surfaces. We answer that we are not against complex surfaces but that there are a lot of people out there who are already doing that very well. We believe that there are unexplored territories which are more fruitful for us to explore. We think there is a void in what we are trying to do.

SJ   There is also a question of how obvious the geometry of a project needs to be. The conditions of abstraction in our work allow us to delay any certain or obvious singular reading of the surface of the project.

ML   We are interested in the projection of something that de-familiarizes you as a prelude to cognition. Abstraction is not understood as reduction, but rather as masking. Our process may be complex and layered but we try to find a synthesis that is more muted in the end. I think that this muteness grants our work some of its characteristic autonomy.

SL   The contemporary parametric and complex surface project may not seek muteness, but they are at the least deeply engaged in alternative theories of design agency. Whether you identify with them or not, you are part of a generation that believes that the death of the author is a good thing or at least that this death is a necessary prelude to the birth of new architectural possibilities.

ML   The parametric school would certainly be a strange bedfellow for us. Its critique of the author probably helps confirm the old adage that all architects are formalists, they just have different ways of lying about it.

BEYOND NEUTRAL BOXES

SL   One of your most constant companions and guarantors of "not-aloneness" is a particular bandwidth of art. Even as one considers an apparently architectural thing, like the box, in relation to your work, it becomes difficult to separate from specific histories of art. The box is a commonplace euphemism for buildings constructed in the modernist idiom. On the other hand, the Los Angeles art movement commonly referred to as Light and Space—which resonates with several aspects of your work—relied heavily on the box. From Larry Bell, who actually made boxes, to James Turrell or Robert Irwin, who cut apertures into building boxes, the Light and Space artists used boxes as the substrate of their production. The box was to their work what flat canvas and paint were to the Abstract Expressionists.

This "architecture of boxes" was concerned with defamiliarizing perception and experience rather than with the construction or building and raises some interesting questions in relation to your work. Your apertures, for example, consistently appear as "familiar" windows. The sense of familiarity derives less from the specifics of their shape or hardware—it does not matter if a particular window is square or double-hung—but rather from the way the apertures frame the view. Your windows obey the rules of Modernist painting: they face the viewer no matter where the viewer happens to be. In their emphatic verticality, they reject all forms of abjection.

Robert Irwin, *1°2°3°4°*, Museum of Contemporary Art, San Diego, 1997.

ML   But the box is not neutral. This discussion of views and apertures in our work cannot be isolated from the expanded spatial landscape defined by form, structure, and sequence. We don't want to control the view or the room in the heroic sense (as did the Light and Space artists) but we want to establish a landscape of experience: "atmospheres" in which the window and the view are only one of many layers. In the View House, the interior and exterior landscapes are visually and physically inflected, reflected and mirrored. The box here is already biased as a result of inclination toward the views and movement. The box is not something we strive for but a norm against which we react. The box is implicated by these explorations of our ambition and the site of the resulting architectural experience.

SL   The box is not neutral for various reasons, but one that is important to this discussion is scale. That the box can easily move from the size of an object to the size of a room to the size of a house gives it not only dimensional flexibility but also tremendous elasticity in its allegiance to a specific medium or disciplinary trajectory. In other words, the box as art and the box as architecture are concepts that are anatomically isomorphic but not necessarily identical in terms of their goals and effects. The boxes of Light and Space relied on the familiarity of the box to produce perceptual and experiential disturbances. Without the clarity of the box to work against, the obscurity of its effects could not be generated.

The question that emerges is if the same can be said of the architectural box. The history of this box is one rooted in the reverse operation: the obfuscation of the contours of the box in favor of experiential clarity. Single rooms, even if very large indeed, as large as Mies' Convention Hall, for example, made it difficult to see the edges of the box in order to make a pure and infinitely visible space inside. Can you make this Modernist and architectural box perform according to the perceptually disturbing goals of the Light and Space box? And is there a point at which the scale or complexity of the box would outpace the value of the box as idea?

SJ   Probably one area of strong difference between our work and the Light and Space artists is that we are very conscious of where we can tightly control conditions in the building design. This allows us to have the confidence to relinquish our hand in other aspects of the project design or execution. We are fascinated by the potential of what can happen within the framework we have shaped. For example, in the gallery building of the Grand Traiano project, we very deliberately introduced a differently scaled curvature to the roof profile to unify the smaller-scaled boxes that appear to be loosely aggregated in the plan. When the boxes themselves become insufficient to address a larger whole, another operation needs to bring coherence. We know that artists and curators will have many different needs for the rooms and the court-yard. The openness in plan allows for flexibility of scale while the sectional roof profile unifies the building.

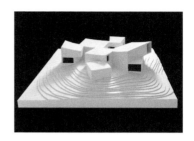

Johnston Marklee, Grand Traiano Art Complex, Gallery, Grottaferrata, Italy, 2007–09.

SL   Billy Al Bengston published an article or, rather, crafted a photographic essay on artist studios in Los Angeles. As a work, its structure is deceptively simple: simple because it seems an utterly prosaic document, describing what were often live-work spaces through dispassionate images and minute and quantifiable data, such as if the room contains traffic noise or not or what kind of light it gets from what kind of window, et cetera. The work is deceptive because it also presents itself as a work, in other words, as a work of art that relies on the isomorphism of art/box and architecture/room in order to explore how they overlap as sites of labor, as sites of production and sites of experience.

The article also raises interesting questions about how boxes are defined through the ways in which they are received. While each room/box differs, they are all consistently photo-graphed with the artist himself (they were all men) clearly on view. On the one hand, this emphatic framing of the artist creates a sense that rather than be self-evident the authority of the artist needs reinforcing through this elaborate staging. On the other hand, it more broadly insists on a connection between an ever-changing set of architectural contexts that are brought into coherence by the presence of the viewing subject. In other words, these boxes do not emerge as art or architecture until they are completed by the viewer and his experience. While your work shares certain formal qualities with the milieu presented in Bengston's essay, notably the simple box at a more or less one room scale that seeks to produce dense experience, I wonder if the viewer solicited by the architectural situations you engender has a similar experience and function.

ML   It is interesting that you come back to Light and Space. Some years ago we helped Robert Irwin on a project in Marfa. As we worked with him, we began to understand how particular he was in dealing with the notion of one room. I never really thought about that in terms of the box, but we certainly learned a lot from him in terms of how a small object could organize a larger field not by spreading out but rather by being very tight and specific. This is particularly interesting when thinking about the Gran Traiano project in Grottaferatta, Italy. Here we are working in a complex semiurban landscape defined by layers of various historic buildings. The new discrete buildings "fit in" by approximating the scale of the surrounding buildings, which vary greatly in size. The distilled building logic is distinct from the context, but also actively transforms the surrounding urban space. Maybe it could be described as operating on two levels simultaneously to create a situation that is both clear and uncertain. Architects don't have the same luxury as artists; we can't demand the same kind of attention from people who just come to look at the work. Architects always work in the context of other forces, such as participants, program, or time. While we profited a lot from the Light and Space artists, we also see the context of art as very different from the context of architecture.

Robert Irwin with Johnston Marklee, project for the Chinati Foundation in Marfa, Texas, 1999–2000.

SL   But there is a circular and sometimes disingenuous way in which architecture uses both its obligations to programs and budgets and clients, as well as its association with art, to remain accountable to neither. This is especially apparent in architecture's relation to Minimalism: architecture has, through a strange kind of magical thinking, managed to turn Minimalism into something that can automatically confirm that the architect has been responsible to his constraints. Minimalism's spatial simplicity is presented as infinitely pliable to program, its limited palette of details is presented as inherently rooted in an economy of means, and its association with good taste means that it is offensive to no client. Minimalism is architecture's Trojan Horse. It is often used as an alibi to allow architects to free themselves of architectural constraints and yet still claim that they are functioning by architectural rules.

The reverse also happens when artists use architecture as a Trojan Horse, as a means to appear as if they are working in social milieu rather than in an autonomous aesthetic realm. Even though artists tend to criticize architects for indulging

Le Corbusier, Ozenfant Studio, Paris, 1922.

their narcissistic impulses rather than restricting themselves to a service profession, when artists look to architecture, they generally don't do so in a way that engages typical architectural constraints conceived in professional terms. These various double standards are systemic, in my view, although they become particularly evident when Minimalism crosses back and forth between mediums, from art to architecture.

One might see this in historical terms as well. The Ozenfant Studio by Le Corbusier is a twentieth-century ground zero for how mediums come together in the box. The studio is as much a cubic form in a still life—in other words, an art box—as it is a space of the free plan, in other words, an architectural box. The toggle between the two is the window, which functions both as a kind of sky painting and as a link to the outside world. However, that link to the outside reveals nothing that might make the world constitute a challenge to the interior. The view offered produces no friction of any kind. The differential relationship to Minimalism explored by art and by architecture hinges on the view out that window: in other words, it hinges on the way different practices construct the real and their relationship to it.

ML Sometimes we talk among ourselves about how we have been labeled as Minimalists. There are good Minimalisms and bad ones. We do not favor John Pawson's restrictive Minimalism. Aldo Rossi or Alvaro Siza, on the other hand, are more generous. In the Ozenfant Studio, the phantom cube is there in the two windows, in the skylight and in the ledge that suggests this extension of the cube. Because the phantom cube is there as a framework, everything else is possible: the stair, the sawtooth skylight, everything.

SJ The cube as a phantom volume has been a driving element in some of the more recent projects. We have described the sensibility of projects like Gran Traiano through an idea of approximation, of using smaller integers and building them up to approximate something altogether different in scale. At the scale of the total form it can be read as a much larger and more complex figure. We paid a lot of attention to individual relationships between the aperture and the singular box. At this larger scale the implied volume morphs into spaces of void and solid within the building mass and in the surrounding urban space. So the role of the phantom volume is transformed by the jump in scale, but is still productive.

SL As you well know, the jump in scale that often happens mid-career has historically been a challenge to architects. Our discussion today coincides with this moment in your career; you too are jumping scales. I am interested in how this general problem posed by changes in the scale of practice intersect with the way you have thus far framed your conceptualization of architectural questions. If your ideas have been structurally dependent on the box as art and box as architecture parallel—an idea that imposes certain limits on size before the analogy breaks down—how will you make this line of speculation expandable?

ML That a change in scale inevitably demands a change in operation is a historical conundrum every architect has had to wrestle with—from Bramante to Mario Botta—with varying degrees of success. We are very much aware of the limitations of scale in the box as a model. As a result, we resort to other architectural elements to bring coherence to larger projects, projects that reach the scale at which the box or the collection of boxes reaches it limitations. The roof as a large figure is such an element and something we have tried since the beginning, from the Palos Verdes Art Center to the Calumet Environmental Center competitions. The roof of the UCLA Graduate Arts Studios and the Menil Drawing Institute have to be understood as extensions and refinements of those earlier endeavors. We have not changed much after fifteen years. Our convictions remain the same. Perhaps what differs today is that our knowledge of their application has grown in scope and precision.

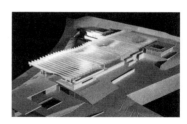

Johnston Marklee, Palos Verdes Art Center, Palos Verdes, California, 2001.

SURFACE VS. MASS

SL Even though James Turrell produced drawings in the context of his installation at the Mendota Hotel, they were made after the fact rather than as a projection of what was to come, or as a set of instructions. In this regard, therefore, and despite the fact that they represent architecture, they are an artist's drawings rather than architectural drawings. On the other hand, they less depict the atmospheric effects of Turrell's manipulations of how light entered the building, which is generally how the "artistic" intentions of the project are understood, than record the movement of light across architectural surfaces. From this point of view, in that they are not only analytic and descriptive but operate through the intersections of lines and surfaces, they speak to conventions of architectural representation.

The digital environment in which architectural drawings are produced today not only has radically altered these conventions but also challenges the way architecture understands its conditions of possibility. For example, someone like Robin Evans could once argue that architecture emerged from the gap between drawing and building but today, as the same digital tools now increasingly control both the construction of the architectural image as well as its built counterpart, this gap is closing. If there is no gap, then from where does architecture spring? One implication that stems from this line of questioning and is pertinent to your current work is that contemporary building technologies allow for construction that is not organized around profiles and contours. It is, in other words, now possible to draw surfaces in a way that does not rely on lines. Form is actually already constructed as a surface. But your work increasingly has neither profile (which is to say it does not proceed by line) nor is determined by surfaces. Instead, it seems to emerge out of a notion of mass, which is an interesting thing to extract from the digital context of architectural design today.

ML Early on we were interested in Alberto Giacometti's drawings—not the single line works but rather the heads composed of multiple lines from which an oscillation of mass and figure and line hold the work together visually. This work challenged us to consider how we might think about mass and form without relying on edges and profiles.

Alberto Giacometti, *Annette*, 1954, oil on canvas (22×29 cm), private collection.

SL But where does the mass come from? What is its point of departure? For example, Gehry would argue, at least preliminarily, that mass is an expression of the volumes required by program. We could contrast this approach with that of John Chamberlain. Both use similar surface treatments, which are always both abject and integral. Both generate simple kinds of shapes or configurations that seem both informal and to in constant search of animation. But if Gehry's mass begins in program, Chamberlain starts with a different conceptual origin. In Chamberlain's sculpture, mass is the result of the manipulation of a material.

SJ The inside and the outside are the same. Similarly, with Claes Oldenburg's soft sculptures, you do not sense that the surface is applied onto a mass but rather feel that it derives from the weight of the mass, slumping.

Claes Oldenburg, *Giant BLT*, 1963, vinyl, kapok fibers, painted wood, and wood, 32 × 39 × 29 in. (81.3 × 99.1 × 73.7 cm).

SL   Yes. But Chamberlain begins with a piece of material as opposed to an image. Furthermore, although the final resting forms of Chamberlain's materials are quite complex, their material homogeneity gives the work a monolithic quality or heaviness, even. Oldenburg's works, on the contrary, are comprised of multiple elements and operations from the image, the material, the entropic sag, et cetera.

SJ   The Hill House is a project that explores these issues in the most direct way. The problem of gravity one faces when building on a hill, as well as all the issues of structure that were a direct consequence, challenged the project. Distilling the design to a limited number of issues is important to our process. The Hill House combines the oppositional qualities of gravity, reminiscent of Richard Serra's work, with aspects of light and buoyancy.

Johnston Marklee, Scope House, Ann Arbor, Michigan, 1999.

SL   Mass does not present itself to the viewer in the same way that the picture plane does. Some of your earlier work toyed with the tension between these two modes of addressing the viewer, with the space between mass and the plane. Some of your more recent work, by contrast, seems to focus more on pictorial questions.

SJ   I think it is interesting to consider mass and porosity and how these conditions affect apertures, structure, and materiality. In the Vault House, qualities of porosity are linked with use and privacy, proximity, view, light, and structure. The overall building mass is more porous on the beach side to the west than on the street side to the east, which is more public.

Achille Castiglioni, project for Casa del Fascio, 1940, model made of cheese.

SL   Rosalind Krauss described Rem Koolhaas's project for the Très Grande Bibliothèque as a piece of Swiss cheese, as a solid and massive block internally riddled and rendered porous by pockets of suspended program. While hers is an evocative description of an important project that initiated a new type of spatial organization, it is not, in fact, an argument rooted in a theory of material or mass. Instead, it recalls Michelangelo, who proceeded by imagining that every block of marble had a figure already in it, a figure that only needed the assistance of a carver to be released. In other words, the stone is a frictionless and ideal piece of matter rather than a resistant and obdurate mass. We could compare this to a project made by the industrial designer Achille Castiglioni for his thesis in architecture school: it was for a Casa del Fascio, for which he made a model out of slabs of cheese. The photographs of this model show the slices slumped in the middle, a little sweaty, as if the model had sat out in the room a bit too long. In other words, the model performs its architecture through a transformative interaction with its environment. The mass of cheese comes alive through its contact with environmental contaminants.

I am curious about how you understand your mass, so to speak, and if you understand your mandate as architects to comprise engaging with, and even encouraging, the environmental exchanges between different forms of contaminants or if you understand your job as protecting the observer from these kinds of potentially toxic or at least deforming exigencies.

ML   This contamination goes back to what you mentioned earlier regarding the erosion of the a priori singular object, whether it is theater or occupancy or material. But you also mentioned a historicism that is very apparent. Instead of starting with heuristic model, we always start projects with something very archetypically architectural. During the process, the heuristic model comes in (like a sponge) and begins to inform the project. We do not feel that we have to follow established rules, but we use historical examples as precedents—a cruciform plan, for instance, is not limited to the function of a church. Our historicism is often convoluted by the heuristic process and the project's limitations. Do you feel this historical interest and perspective on our work is a certain burden?

SL   It is a constraining factor. But, on the other hand, constraints are your strength; they are what you need. Familiarity is a complicated thing. Familiarity can easily become unfamiliar.

ML   Do you mean how a sign in the postmodern sense can take on multiple readings? I would agree that the constraint of any project provides a specific and somewhat unfamiliar context to a concept that might be otherwise familiar.

SL   Today, rather than make assertive manifestos or act out critical rejections, we sift, we sort, we scan. These are fundamentally new ways of organizing the world that are rooted in much more provisional epistemologies. Over the past fifty years we have been developing tools in order to prepare us to work in this new context. Learning to understand the sign as engendering multiple meanings is one such tool. Typology and the diagram are also systems for organizing information into loose and flexible systems. The model offered by these various lineages is more toolkit than historical precedent.

ML   For us, type is a toolkit and not a membership card to a certain lineage. When we think about projects, we do not necessarily have to look at courtyard types as an evolution of a certain historical lineage. We look for what we can gain from the type itself. Our education at Harvard's Graduate School of Design left us very self-conscious about this association with historical type. But I think we are also critical of the typical GSD models, whether formulated in the seventies or the eighties. The school usually boasts a profile of architects that cover all the grounds and are everywhere but nowhere. I am even thinking of the postmodern phase before now: a little bit parametric, a little bit typological, a little bit historical. I think when we talk about our own practice we are very conscious not to default to that agenda.

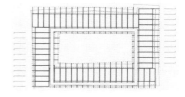

Mark Lee, B-A-S-E-L Housing, Studio Herzog & de Meuron, Harvard GSD, 1994.

Office of Johnston Marklee, Los Angeles, 2014.

Ed Ruscha, *Every Building on the Sunset Strip*, 1966, 54 pages, accordion fold, black and white photographic illustrations (18 × 14.2 cm).

sL   Having a little bit of everything in order to satisfy the market is not the same as having a collection, although the distinction between the two is pliable. I think of you as collectors. You collect things, chairs, books, clothing and you collect knowledge and especially erudition, erudition in the form of obscure anecdotes from the history of architecture. While the postmodern impulse toward the historical combined with its impulse toward the superficial yielded a tendency towards connoisseurship, I find it more productive to think about this in terms of contemporary approaches to data and information. Cataloging is a primary feature of today's cognitive mapping but instead of producing map it just produces more catalog entries.

A good example of the implications we can extract from this kind of operation today can be found in Ed Ruscha's serial photographs. Even though his works are serial, things theoretically without end, he always constructs hypothetical limits and systems of restraint to contain the series: *every* building on the sunset strip or *thirty-four* parking lots, no more or no less. Today, we would struggle with whether and how to invent those limits. Today we would make a catalog rather than an art book, a wiki rather than a map. Furthermore, the term that has been used to describe the individual photographs in a Ruscha series is "indifferent." In his work, it might be necessary that there are specifically thirty-four parking lots, but it doesn't much matter which particular parking lots are included or even who took the photographs themselves. Your work has important connections with these issues except you catalog rather than produce series, and your entries seem less to betray indifference than to demonstrate decorum.

ML   There is an analogy to pornography. You either resist pornography and attempt to abstain or you say okay to pornography and you orgasm. I think the decorum we are describing is like that. Another way to think about decorum, and this is what we favor, would be to imagine it as a practice that balances competing desires for ambition and propriety. These factors are not resolved to be static as in good behavior. You seem to be asking, is our work subversive enough? But maybe decorum is washing out our desire to do subversive work and tempering our desire for abjection.

SL   But the more important question is not how do you respond to pornography but how do you define it? Choosing whether to be subversive or not is already to accept given notions of the proper. The legal definition of pornography, rooted in the notion of "I can't define what it is but I know it when I see it," sanctions that worst kind of tyranny by consensus. Architecture is a compelling field because it is ideally situated to test the limits or to redirect this kind of thinking.

What I mean by this might become clear if we compare Diderot's letter to the blind to the Indian proverb of the blind men and the elephant. In the Indian proverb, seven blind men touch the same elephant but they all "see" a different elephant. This is a story about the essential and distinguishing nature of experience. Diderot, on the other hand, argues that if seven blind men touch this elephant they would all "see" exactly the same thing because he understood vision to be completely overdetermined. If your work is the elephant, what would the blind men see? Or rather, what kind of experience and form of perception do you intend to solicit from your viewer? Neither the Indian proverb nor Diderot's letter can be reduced to a simple form of subversion or acceptance but, on the other hand, neither particularly suits our current cultural situation. We cannot accept the former's essentialism and have grown resistant to the latter's logocentrism. I hope that contemporary architecture will sharpen its interest in questions of experience and perception so that they more explicitly help us resolve this dilemma. As your work unfolds it will be interesting to observe the matchup between material sag and conceptual gravitas.

ML   This seems to be on many peoples' minds. We always think the question of what is next is partly contrived and that it has actually been on the table from the beginning. We do not see our work developing in a linear way as we consider what we have built, in part because we see the future in terms of our community as a landscape of possibilities. We appreciate these questions because they remind us why we are so fascinated by the work of contemporary artists Peter Fischli and David Weiss. In their Visible World series we admire the intensity, time, and respect they give to everyday places and circumstances. The matter-of-fact nature of the images balances the ordinary with the extraordinary and reveals a level of latent intensity that has great potential for invention in contemporary architecture.

I think our work aspires to this ordinary extraordinary, which is one way that we stand out as architects and as artists, who are all more often interested in being extraordinary. But we also remain open to the possibility that we will not always do things exactly the way we do them now. As a practice, we have remained deliberately agile in terms of our approach to scale, to clients, to form; we are not nostalgic or especially loyal to the earlier phases of our practice because we are not especially interested in reliving that work or in being devoted to some pure, original objective. The room and the window are still on our minds, but it is a new room, a different room, and the window has shifted.

sj   To conclude, I am curious how you, as a scholar, see our current work in relation to that of our colleagues.

sl   One feature of the contemporary landscape, of its culture of churning and sorting, is that nothing really stands out or has priority. We no longer insist on a clear division between background or foreground buildings and instead seem to produce a tremendous amount of middle ground chatter. As a scholar of the contemporary, as you put it, my proclivity would be to observe the landscape as a whole and to resist the temptation to focus on discrimination. One immediate thing this form of observation makes evident is that architects themselves are not insisting on standing out as they once did. This reticence takes many forms, from buildings that are decorous rather than subversive to discourse that is often more like shop talk than a manifesto. Architects are increasingly silent regarding the stakes of what they do.

ml   But do we have to speak? Or can our not saying be a way of saying?

sl   By asking me, you are "saying," even if only by way of trying to get me to say it for you. Perhaps this is another technique for producing architecture that is not alone.

This text is based on a conversation held in Los Angeles on November 19, 2011.

Vault House

DESIGN YEARS
2008–2010

CONSTRUCTION YEARS
2011–2013

LOCATION
Oxnard, California, United States

SITE AREA
929 m² / 10,000 sf

FLOOR AREA
334 m² / 3,600 sf

CLIENT
Steven and Jerri Nagelberg

PRINCIPALS
Sharon Johnston and Mark Lee

PROJECT TEAM
Katrin Terstegen, Andri Luescher, Nicholas
Hofstede, Anna Neimark, Anton Schneider,
Yoshi Nagamine, Ryan Roettker

STRUCTURAL ENGINEER
William Koh and Associates

CONTRACTOR
RJP Construction

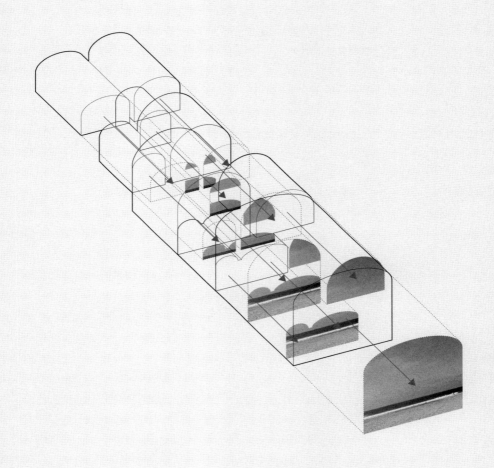

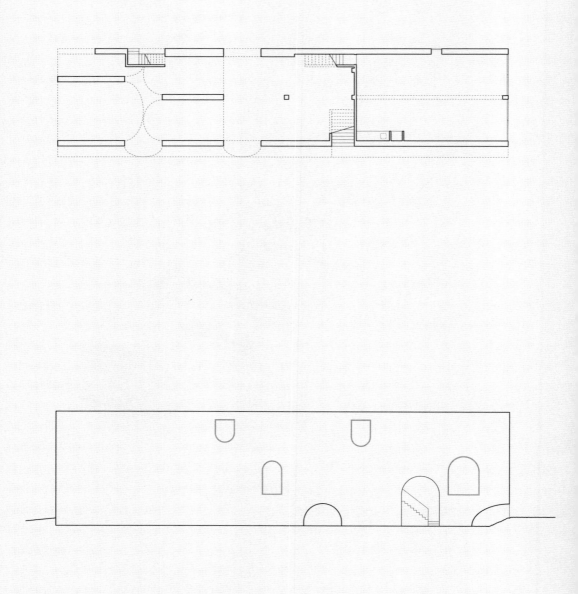

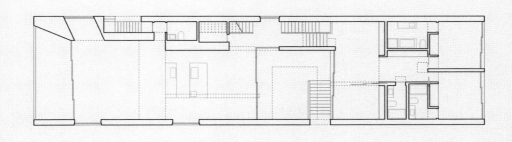

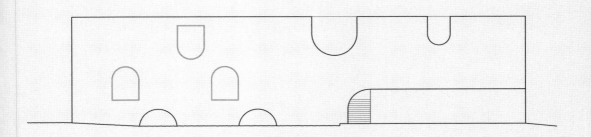

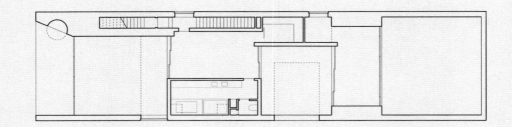

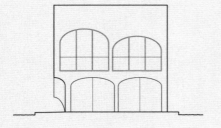

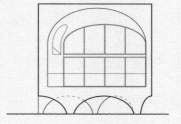

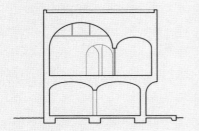

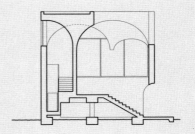

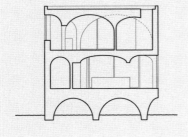

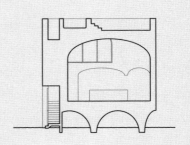

Appendix

Works
1999–2017

1999
Scope House
Ann Arbor, Michigan

1999
Eroshevich Car Port
Studio City, California

1999
Hotel Pro Forma
Orestad, Denmark

1999
Keely Weatherford House
Hollywood, California

1999
Mameg I
Brentwood, California

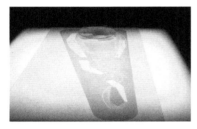

2000
TKTS Kiosk
New York City, New York

2000
UCLA Perloff Hall Lab
Los Angeles, California

2000–2001
Lannan Foundation Writers
Studio
Marfa, Texas

2000
Penner House
Palm Springs, California

2000–2002
Marfa House 3
Marfa, Texas

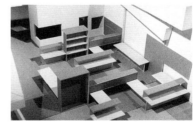

2000
Kick Media
Culver City, California

2000–2002
Mound House
Marfa, Texas

2000
Earl Jean Photographic Studio
Los Angeles, California

2000–2004
Hill House
Pacific Palisades, California

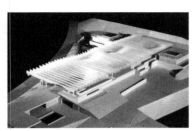

2001
Palos Verdes Art Center
Palos Verdes, California

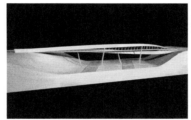

2001
Wildwood Pedestrian Bridge
Wildwood, Missouri

2001–2005
Nano at LACMA Lab
Los Angeles, California

2001–2003
Walden Wilson Studio
Culver City, California

2001–2002
UCLA Perloff Hall
Resource Room
Los Angeles, California

2001–2002
UCLA Perloff Hall Gallery
Los Angeles, California

2001–2004
Sale House
Venice, California

2001–2002
Corrine Seeds University
Elementary School North Yard
Los Angeles, California

2001
Marfa Public Library
Marfa, Texas

2002
San Jose Museum of Art
San Jose, California

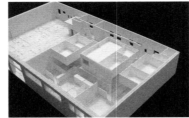

2002
Skid Row Housing Trust
Los Angeles, California

2002
Building Study for Robert Irwin
Marfa, Texas

2002–2004
Standard 8 Offices
Los Angeles, California

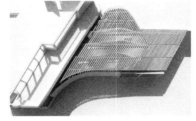

2002
Hewitt Residence
Los Angeles, California

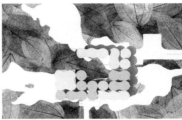

2003
Ford Calumet Competition
Chicago, Illinois

2003
Bitel Mancall Residence
Bel Air, California

2003
Korean Cultural Center
Tokyo, Japan

2003–2005
Amiryani Studio
Marfa, Texas

2004
Architecture Foundation
Headquarters
Los Angeles, California

2004
Screen (Documentary Film
Theater)
Los Angeles, California

2004–2005
Eliel-Muller Residence
Los Angeles, California

2004–2005
Hungry Cat
Hollywood, California

2004–2006
The Orchid
Santa Monica, California

2005
SCPR / KPCC Headquarters
Pasadena, California

2005
Pool House
Los Angeles, California

2005
Whalen Residence
Santa Monica, California

2005
Linda Loudermilk
Los Angeles, California

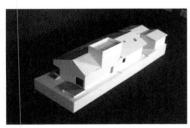

2005
Howard Residence
Venice, California

2005–2009
View House, in collaboration
with Diego Arraigada
Rosario, Argentina

2005–2006
Bandini Gallery
Culver City, California

2005
Luu Residence
Kauai, Hawaii

2006
Hong Kong Design Institute
Hong Kong, China

2006
Project Row House
Houston, Texas

2006–2007
Hungry Cat
Santa Barbara, California

2006
Critical Mass, Fringe
Tijuana, Mexico

2006
San Vitores Plaza
Tuman, Guam

2006–2007
Thirsty Cat Restaurant
Hollywood, California

2006
Michaelson Residence
Marina del Rey, California

2006–2007
Mameg II
Beverly Hills, California

2006–2007
Maison Martin Margiela
Beverly Hills, California

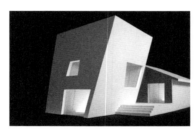

2006
Spath-Zakkour Residence
Venice, California

2006–2007
Helios House, in collaboration
with Office dA
Los Angeles, California

2007
MOCA Fresh
Los Angeles, California

2007
Honor Fraser
Culver City, California

2007
Aohai New Town
Aohai, China

2007
Walk Through History
Portimao, Portugal

2007
Murakami: Kaikai Kiki
Merchandise Room, MOCA
Los Angeles, California

2007–2008
Simchowitz House
Los Angeles, California

2007
Energy Store
Los Angeles, California

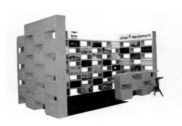

2007
BP Power Station Traveling
Stand
New Orleans, Louisiana

2007–2008
Take-a-Bao
Century City, California

2007–2008
Roberts & Tilton Gallery
Culver City, California

2007–2009
Windward School Gallery
Los Angeles, California

2007–2008
Grimes Residence
Malibu, California

2007
Metro Southeast Corridor
Stations
Houston, Texas

2008
No Room Exhibition
Christopher Grimes Gallery
Santa Monica, California

2007–2009
Gran Traiano Art Complex
(GTAC)
Grottaferrata, Italy

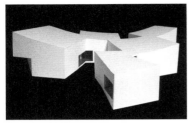

2007–2009
GTAC, Gallery
Grottaferrata, Italy

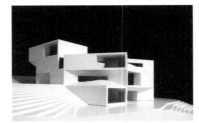

2007–2009
GTAC, Stack House
Grottaferrata, Italy

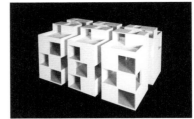

2007–2009
GTAC, Housing
in collaboration with HHF
Grottaferrata, Italy

2008–2009
"One Variation in Five Parts"
at Syracuse University
Syracuse, New York

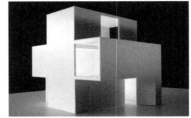

2008
Cross House
Los Angeles, California

2008
House House
Ordos, Inner Mongolia

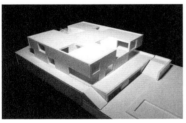

2008
Carmelina House
Brentwood, California

2008
Poggio Golo Winery
Montepulciano, Italy

2008
Steinman Residence
Malibu, California

2008–2013
Vault House
Oxnard, California

2008
Paper Pop-Up
Los Angeles, California

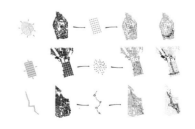

2009
Portugal Arte
Lisbon, Portugal

2009
Melides House
Melides, Portugal

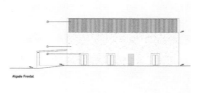

2009
Azinheira Houses
Grandola, Portugal

2009–2010
Momed
Beverly Hills, California

2009
William Rast Store
Century City, California

2009–2010
Later Layer
Italian Cultural Institute
Los Angeles, California

2009–2010
The Hundreds Store
New York, New York

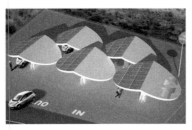

2009
Ecotality Prototype
California

2009–2011
Baxter-Hodiak Residence
Los Angeles, California

2009
Court House
En Sully, Switzerland

2010
White Cube Green Maze
Exhibition, Carnegie Foundation
Pittsburgh, Pennsylvania

2010
Material Pictures
Culver City, California

2010
Standbad Mythenquai
Zurich, Switzerland

2010–2016
Ark House
Pacific Palisades, California

2010–2014
Hut House
Kauai, Hawaii

2010–2011
Chan Luu Showroom
Los Angeles, California

2010–2011
Any House is a Home
Peabody Essex Museum
Salem, Massachusetts

2011
Chile House
Penco, Chile

2011–2012
Palo Vista Residence
Los Angeles, California

2011–2013
Porch House
Los Angeles, California

2011–2019
UCLA Graduate Art Studios
Culver City, California

2011
University of Southern
California (USC)
Los Angeles, California

2011
1787, Hong Kong-Shenzhen
Biennale
Shenzhen, China

2011
Chan Luu Showroom
New York, New York

2011
Club House 1,2,3
Ingrina, Portugal

2011–2012
Arcana Bookstore
Culver City, California

2012
Lapis Press
Culver City, California

2012–2014
Six Pieds Trois Pouces
Paris, France

2012–2017
Solo House
Cretas, Spain

2012
Stavros Merjos Limited
Beverly Hills, California

2012–2014
11520 San Vicente
Los Angeles, California

2012–2013
Everything Loose Will Land
MAK Center
Los Angeles, California

2012–2017
Menil Drawing Institute
Houston, Texas

2012–2015
Sterling Ruby Studio
Vernon, California

2012–2015
Tisch Gallery
Beverly Hills, California

2012–2013
Velvet Store
Brentwood, California

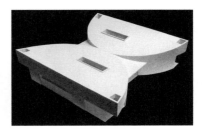

2012
But House
Malibu, California

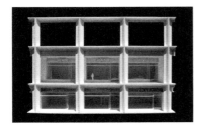

2012–2017
Miami Design District
Miami, Florida

2013–2016
Menil Energy House
Houston, Texas

2013
Pavilion of Six Views
Shanghai, China

2013
James Welling: Monograph
Hammer Museum
Los Angeles, California

2013–2016
Aesop, in collaboration with
MG&Co.
Culver City, California

2013–2018
Amalfi Residence
Los Angeles, California

2013
Forest City
Los Angeles, California

2013–2014
Various Small Fires
Los Angeles, California

2013
San Rafael House
Los Angeles, California

2014
Apparition, Hammer Museum
Los Angeles, California

2014
Robert Heinecken:
Object Matter, Hammer Museum
Los Angeles, California

2014
Harvard Laboratories
Cambridge, Massachusetts

2014
Naturhistorisches Museum
In collaboration with HHF
Basel, Switzerland

2014
Chan Luu Showroom Tokyo
Tokyo, Japan

2014
Velvet NYC
New York, New York

2014–2015
Aesop
Santa Monica, California

2015
Cleto Murano Credenza

2015
MCA Masterplan
Chicago, Illinois

2015–2017
MCA Restaurant and
Renovation
Chicago, Illinois

2015
Chicago Architecture Biennial,
Chicago Cultural Center
Chicago, Illinois

2015
MCA
Chicago, Illinois

2015–2017
Lisbon Architecture Triennale
Lisbon, Portugal

2015
MOCA Los Angeles
Los Angeles, California

2015
Green Line Arts Center
Chicago, Illinois

Contributors

SHARON JOHNSTON

is founder and Partner of Johnston Marklee & Associates. She studied history and art history at Stanford University and architecture at the Harvard Graduate School of Design. She has lectured widely and has served on the board of the American Institute of Architects. She has taught at Harvard University, UCLA, Rice University, and the Southern California Institute of Architecture.

WALEAD BESHTY

is an artist and writer working in Los Angeles. He is Associate Professor at Art Center College of Design in Pasadena.

BLESS

is a fashion and design studio, founded in 1997 by Ines Kaag and Desiree Heiss and with shops in Berlin and Paris. Their independent working method often involves collaboration with customers and friends in fashion, art, design, and architecture. They have participated in exhibitions at the Art Institute of Chicago, MAK Vienna, the 2014 Istanbul Design Biennial, and Centre Pompidou-Metz.

VERONIKA KELLNDORFER

is a Berlin-based artist who examines the intersection between architectural objects and social space. She has received numerous grants, including residencies at Villa Massimo, Rome (2005) and the Goethe-Institut in Kyoto (2012). Her work has been most recently exhibited in solo shows at Christopher Grimes Gallery in Santa Monica, the Pinakothek der Moderne in Munich, and the Instituto Lina Bo Bardi in São Paulo.

LIVIA CORONA

is a photographer based in New York and Mexico City. Her work has been exhibited worldwide, including at the New Museum New York, the Bronx Museum of the Arts, and the Museo Tamayo in Mexico City. She was a 2009 Guggenheim Fellow and 2013 Pictet Prix Nominee. Her two monographs, titled *Enanitos Toreros* and *Of People and Houses,* were published in 2008 and 2009 respectively.

LUISA LAMBRI

is a Los Angeles-based artist born in Como, Italy. Her work has been exhibited in museums worldwide, including at the Barbican Centre, London; the Hammer Museum and the J. Paul Getty Museum, Los Angeles; the New Museum and Guggenheim Museum in New York; the Carnegie Museum of Art, Pittsburgh; and at the Museum of Contemporary Art, Chicago. In 2004, the Menil Collection in Houston organized her first survey exhibition.

RETO GEISER

is an architect and scholar of modern architecture with a focus on the intersections between architecture, pedagogy, and media. He is the Gus Wortham Assistant Professor at the Rice University School of Architecture. A founding principal of the design practice MG&Co., he develops spatial strategies on scales from the book to the house.

SYLVIA LAVIN

is a Professor of Architectural History and Theory at UCLA, where she served as Chair of Architecture and Urban Design from 1996–2006. Her books include *Form Follows Libido: Architecture and Richard Neutra in a Psychoanalytic Culture* (2005), *Kissing Architecture* (2011), and *Flash in the Pan* (2014). She curated the 2013 exhibition "Everything Loose Will Land" at the MAK Center in Los Angeles.

MARK LEE

is a founder and Partner of Johnston Marklee & Associates. He studied architecture at the University of Southern California and at the Harvard Graduate School of Design. His writing has appeared in *Werk, Bauen + Wohnen, Daidalos, San Rocco,* and *Dédalo.* He has taught at Harvard University, UCLA, ETH Zurich, Rice University, and the Technical University of Berlin.

MARIANNE MUELLER

is a Zurich-based artist, mostly working with photography, video, installation, and books. She collects observations of quotidian environments that she recontextualizes in her works, often in reaction to the specific site of an exhibition. She is a professor at the Zurich University of the Arts. Her publications include *The Flock* (2004), *The Proper Ornaments* (2008), and *Stairs Etc.* (2014).

JACK PIERSON

is an artist in New York. He studied at Massachusetts College of Art and Design, and his work is in the collections of the Metropolitan Museum of Art, the Whitney Museum, the Guggenheim Museum, and the San Francisco Museum of Modern Art, among others. He is currently publishing an artist's book called *Tomorrow's Man.*

RAYMUND RYAN

is Curator of the Heinz Architectural Center at the Carnegie Museum of Art in Pittsburgh, Pennsylvania. He was first the Irish Commissioner for the Venice Architecture Biennale. His publications include *Cool Construction* (2001), *Michael Maltzan: Alternate Ground* (2005), *Gritty Brits: New London Architecture* (2007), and *White Cube, Green Maze: New Art Landscapes* (2012).

PHILIP URSPRUNG

is Professor of the History of Art & Architecture at ETH Zurich. He previously taught at the University of Zurich, Columbia University, and the Barcelona Institute of Architecture. He is the editor of *Herzog & de Meuron: Natural History* (2002) and the author of *Allan Kaprow, Robert Smithson, and the Limits to Art* (2013).

NICOLÁS VALENTINI

is a filmmaker and actor based in Rosario, Argentina. He is the scriptwriter, producer, and codirector of *4 3 2 UNO* (2009) and the documentary *Pañuelos para la historia* (2013). His short films include *Eterno Desvelar* (2009), *El Visitante* (2009), and *Maní* (2007). His work has been screened at international film festivals, including Mar del Plata, Lisbon, Leipzig, Cairo, Chennai, Shanghai, and has received numerous distinctions.

JAMES WELLING

is a photographer based in Los Angeles and New York. He studied at the California Institute of the Arts and is a Professor in the Department of Art at UCLA. A retrospective of his work, entitled *James Welling: Monograph,* was exhibited at the Cincinnati Art Museum in 2013.

SARAH WHITING

is Dean of the Rice University School of Architecture and Partner of WW Architecture. Her writing has been published widely and she is the editor of *Differences: Topographies of Contemporary Architecture; Beyond Surface Appeal: Literalism, Sensibilities, and Constituencies in the Work of James Carpenter* and the *POINT* series from Princeton University Press.

Acknowledgments

This book is a collective effort almost as long in the making as any of the houses it presents. What began as a casual conversation among friends at a Zurich café, and took further shape in Houston, turned into a manifold publication project that would have not been possible without the dedication, intelligence, criticism, and generosity of the whole team involved.

We would like to thank a group of exceptionally talented and smart friends and colleagues for the generous contributions that form the core of this book: Walead Beshty, Livia Corona, Desiree Heiss and Ines Kaag (BLESS), Veronika Kellndorfer, Luisa Lambri, Sylvia Lavin, Marianne Mueller, Jack Pierson, Raymund Ryan, Philip Ursprung, Nicolás Valentini, James Welling, and Sarah Whiting.

Despite the rapidly changing conditions in the publishing world, David Marold, our editor, has shown remarkable commitment to this project. We would like to express our gratitude for his enduring patience and persistent belief in this endeavor. Angelika Heller at Birkhäuser offered crucial support in materializing the book. Rachel Julia Engler's sharp pen in the copy editing process and Amelia Hazinski's exactitude in proofreading were invaluable.

At Johnston Marklee, Lindsay Erickson has been instrumental in keeping the project on track, bypassing the daily "distractions" of architectural practice and helping to connect the dots. We are grateful for her rigor, commitment, and patience. Taryn Bone took on the arduous task of chasing down a great number of image rights holders. Nicholas Hofstede, Andri Luescher, Anton Schneider, Roldolfo Dias, Katrin Terstegen, Rossana Jimenez, Jeff Mikolajewski, and Mary Casper, and our many other collaborators over the years, have been integral in shaping the work presented on these pages.

At MG&Co., Mary Casper, Amelia Hazinski, Alicia Hergenroeder, Kelsey Olafson, Mahan Shirazi, and Louie Weiss have been involved at different stages and in different aspects of the book. We would like to thank them for their enthusiasm. A special gratitude extends to Noëmi Mollet for her continuing encouragement, criticism, and advice, and for visually mastering the different voices in this volume.

Scott Colman and Keith Mitnick provided invaluable critical feedback.

Finally, we thank our families, who shared both the stresses and the inspirations of this project.

R.G./S.J./M.L.

Johnston Marklee Collaborators Since 1998

Jeffery Adams, Shin Ah, Paul Andersen, Toni-Maria Anschuetz, Diego Arraigada, Andrew Ashey, James Backwell, Mark Rea Baker, Bettina Baumberger, Mie Benson, David Benjamin, Aaron Bentley, Kateryna Bilyk, Taryn Bone, Emmanuelle Bourlier, Philipp Breuer, Laurel Broughton, Brennan Buck, Nelson Byun, Nadia Carassai, Alessandro Carrea, Mary Casper, Gabriel Chareton, Albert Chu, Michelle Cintron, Josh Coggeshall, Matthew Coogan, Fiona Cuypers-Stanieda, Michael deJong, Rodolfo Reis Dias, Vy Drouin-Le, Lindsay Erickson, Amber Evans, Zarah Fahrni, Nefer Fernandez, Yvonne Fissel, Robert Garlipp, Letizia Garzoli, Matthew Gillis, Amalia Gonzales-Dahl, Iris Gramegna, Joanna Grant, David Gray, Grete Grubelich, Brian Ha, Evan Hall, Leila Hamidi, Joanna Hankamer, Doug Harsevoort, Anna Hermann, David Himelman, Nicholas Hofstede, Lars Holt, Ruth Hügli, Peder Vilnes Jahnsen, Rossana Jimenez, Sharon Johnston, Elizabeth Jones, Austin Kaa, Howard Kang, Andrew Kao, Daveed Kapoor, Mehr Khanpour, Nathan Kiebler, Alice Ko, Maximillian Kocademirci, Gary Ku, Clover Lee, Jungwoo Lee, Mark Lee, Channa Levy, Zeheng Li, Meghan Lloyd, Andri Luescher, Lorenzo Marasso, Ellen Marsh, Paruyr Matevosyan, Anna Meloyan, Mark Mendez, Owen Merrick, Jeffery Mikolajewski, Midori Mizuhara, Amanda Moschel, Yoshi Nagamine, Anna Neimark, Grace Pei, Thibaut Pierron, Mihai Radulescu, Jonathan Raz, Claudia Reisenberger, Alan Ricks, Florian Ringli, Aleris Rodgers, Ryan Roettker, Anne Rosenberg, Juan Salazar, Anton Schneider, James Schrader, Ian Searcy, Bradley Silling, Joshua Stein, Lorenzo Stieger, Danielle Tellez, Regina Teng, Katrin Terstegen, Martin Tessarz, Ian Thomas, Mike Todd, Antonio Torres, Sidian Tu, Francesco Valenta-Gorjup, Nazifa Virani, Charlotte von Moos, Anna Walling, Isabell Wolke, Karl Wruck, Lorena Yamamoto, William Zyck

Image Credits

© 2015 Artists Rights Society (ARS), New York/SIAE, Rome. Giorgio de Chirico, *Melancholia*, dated 1916, painted ca. 1940, oil on canvas, 20×26.5 in. (50.8×67.3 cm): 70

© John Baldessari, *Crowd with Shape of Reason Missing: Example 1*, 2012, Mixografia print on handmade paper, 30 × 43 inches. Published by Mixografia, Los Angeles, Edition of 60: 30B

© Walead Beshty: 187–198

© Maria Ida Biggi, Giacinta Manfredi: 70

© BLESS, courtesy of Ines Kaag and Desiree Heiss: 218, 219 bottom, 220–223, 227 bottom, 228, 229

© The Trustees of the British Museum: 107

© Chris Burden. Chris Burden, *Metropolis II*, Los Angeles County Museum of Art, 2012. Courtesy of the Nicolas Berggruen Charitable Foundation: 164 top

© Kristin M. Burke: 225 center and bottom

© Mario Carrieri: 77

© Chicago History Museum, HB-26823, Hedrich-Blessing, photographer: 162 top

© Collection Centre Canadien d'Architecture/Canadian Centre for Architecture, Montreal. John Hejduk fonds: 174

© Collection Centre Canadien d'Architecture/Canadian Centre for Architecture, Montreal. James Stirling/Michael Wilford fonds: 172

© Livia Corona, images courtesy of the artist and Parque Galeria: 50–63

Courtesy of Editoriale Domus. Domus 610, October 1980: 75

© Fondazione Achille Castiglioni, Milan: 267

Courtesy Fondazione Centro Internazionale Di Studi Di Architettura Andrea Palladio: 73

© Eisenman Architects: 76

© EPA/CHRISTIAN ESCOBAR MORA/Corbis: 226

© Eredi Aldo Rossi: 175

© F.L.C./ADAGP, Paris/Artists Rights Society (ARS), New York 2015, Le Corbusier: 264

© Gehry Partners, LLP: 66, 75, 118

© 2015 Alberto Giacometti Estate/Licensed by VAGA and ARS, New York, NY. Alberto Giacometti, *Annette*, 1954, oil on canvas (22×29 cm), Private Collection: 266 top

© gta Archives, ETH Zurich. Heinrich Bernhard Hoesli Papers: 68

© gta Archives, ETH Zurich. Ernst Gisel Papers (Photo: Georg Gisel): 34D

© 2015 Robert Irwin/Artists Rights Society (ARS), New York, © Pablo Mason. Robert Irwin, *1°2°3°4°*, Museum of Contemporary Art, San Diego, 1997. Photo by Pablo Mason: 261

© Veronika Kellndorfer, images courtesy of the artist and Christopher Grimes Gallery: 146–159

© Johnston Marklee: 30C, 34E, 34F, 34G, 38H, 38I, 38J, 38K, 40, 44M, 44P, 74, 106, 107, 108 center, 109 top, 112 top and center, 114, 167, 258, 259, 262, 263, 265, 267, 269 top and center, gatefolds

© Johnston Marklee. Photo: Miljenko Bernfest: 106 top

© Johnston Marklee. Photo: Gustavo Frittegotto: 163

© Johnston Marklee and Walead Beshty. Photo: Fredrik Nilsen: 116, 219 top

© Johnston Marklee and Julius Schulman: 30A, 112, 113 bottom, 227 top

© Johnston Marklee and Eric Staudenmaier: 107 center, 108 top, 110, 164 bottom, 169, 224, 225 top

© Lacaton & Vassal Architectes. Photo: Phillipe Ruault: 75

© Luisa Lambri: 131–141

© J. Mayer H. und Partner, Architekten. Photo: Jesko M. Johnsson-Zahn: 76

© MG&Co./Noëmi Mollet and Reto Geiser: 106 bottom, 108 bottom, 167 top, 219 center

© Marianne Mueller: 1–22, 299–320, front and back endpapers

© Office for Metropolitan Architecture (OMA): 73, 162 bottom, 165

© 1963 Claes Oldenburg. Claes Oldenburg, *Giant BLT*, 1963, vinyl, kapok fibers, painted wood, and wood, 32×39×29 in. (81.3×99.1×73.7 cm). Whitney Museum of American Art, New York; gift of The American Contemporary Art Foundation Inc., Leonard A. Lauder, President 2002.244a-s: 266

© Murai Osamu: 109

© Jack Pierson, courtesy of the artist and Cheim&Read, New York: 243–255

© Robert Rauschenberg Foundation/Licensed by VAGA, New York, NY. Robert Rauschenberg, *Dirt Painting (for John Cage)*. Detail, ca.1953, dirt and mold in wood box, 15.5×16×2.5 inches (39.4×40.6×6.4 cm). Robert Rauschenberg Foundation: 69

© Ed Ruscha 429.2008.a-bbb. Edward Ruscha, *Every Building on the Sunset Strip 1966*, 54 pages (folded), black & white photographic illustrations; accordion fold; original slipcase, silver paper over boards; white paper belly band, 18×14.2cm. Art Gallery of New South Wales. Purchased with funds provided by the Photography Collection Benefactors' Program 2008. Photo: AGNSW: 269 bottom

© Studio Michael Schoner: 115

© Julius Schulman: 113 top

© Nicolás Valentini: 90–103

© James Welling: 44N, 440, 202–215

EDITOR
Reto Geiser

CONCEPT
Johnston Marklee and MG&Co.

PROJECT TEAM (JML + MG&CO.)
Taryn Bone, Mary Casper, Lindsay Erickson,
Amelia Hazinski, Mahan Shirazi, Louie Weiss

COPY EDITING
Rachel Julia Engler, New York

PROOF READING
Amelia Hazinski, Houston

DESIGN AND TYPESETTING
MG&Co., Houston
Noëmi Mollet and Reto Geiser

LITHOGRAPHY
Pixelstorm, Vienna

PRINTING AND BINDING
Kösel GmbH & Co. KG, Altusried-Krugzell

TYPE
Executive (Gavillet & Rust)

PAPER
Lessebo Design Rough White 100 g/m²
Magno Gloss 135 g/m²
Munken Polar Rough 300 g/m²

Printed on acid-free paper produced
from chlorine-free pulp. TCF ∞

Printed in Germany

Library of Congress Cataloging-in-
Publication data. A CIP catalog record for
this book has been applied for at
the Library of Congress.

Bibliographic information published by
the German National Library: The German
National Library lists this publication in the
Deutsche Nationalbibliografie. Detailed bibliographic data are available on the Internet
at http://dnb.dnb.de.

This work is subject to copyright. All rights
are reserved, whether the whole or part of
the material is concerned, specifically the
rights of translation, reprinting, re-use of
illustrations, recitation, broadcasting, repro-
duction on microfilms or in other ways, and
storage in databases. For any kind of use,
permission of the copyright owner must
be obtained.

Artworks © 2016 by the artists
Texts © 2016 by the authors

© 2017 Birkhäuser Verlag GmbH, Basel
P.O. Box 44, 4009 Basel, Switzerland
Part of Walter de Gruyter GmbH, Berlin/
Boston

For copyright of illustrations and photographs, see the detailed list in the appendix.
Every reasonable attempt has been made
to identify all copyright holders. Errors or
omissions will be corrected in subsequent
editions.

ISBN 978-3-0356-1485-5   2. Edition
ISBN 978-3-99043-489-5   1. Edition

9 8 7 6 5 4 3 2

www.birkhauser.com

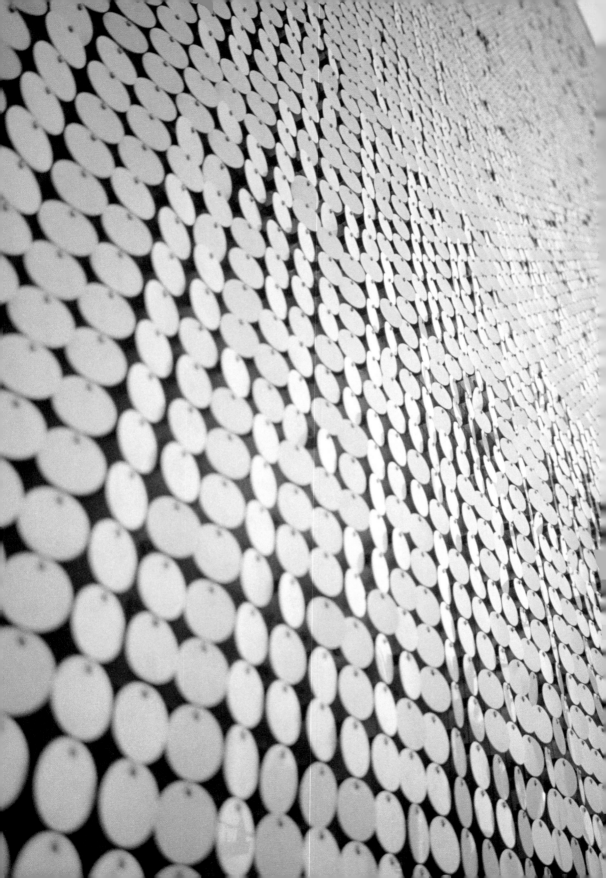

DREAM

No Smoking
---- *Please* ----

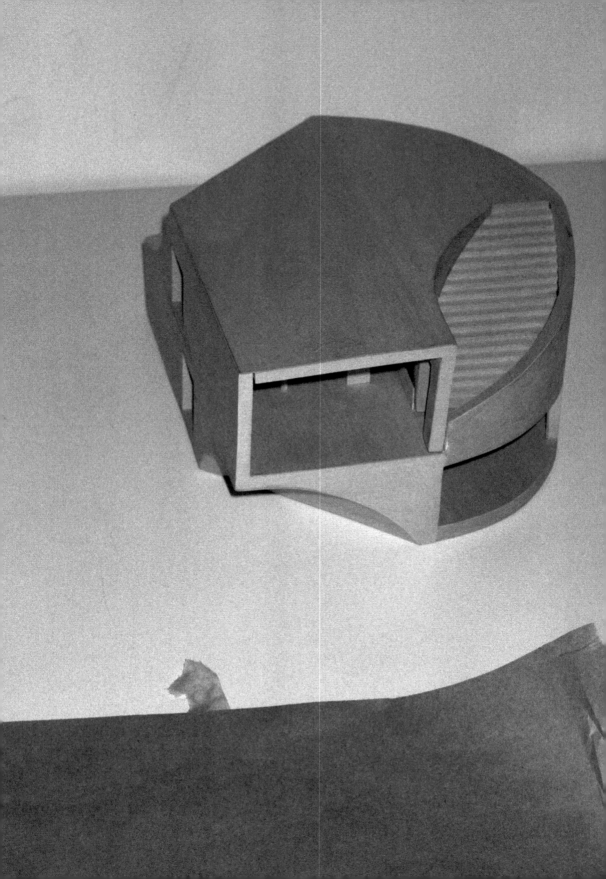